Red Flower, Green Leaf

A True Story of Love,
Faithfulness, and Answered Prayer

HEATHER NELSON

WESTBOW
PRESS®
A DIVISION OF THOMAS NELSON
& ZONDERVAN

This book is a work of non-fiction. Unless otherwise noted, the author
and the publisher make no explicit guarantees as to the accuracy of
the information contained in this book and in some cases, names of
people and places have been altered to protect their privacy.

WestBow Press books may be ordered through booksellers or by contacting:

WestBow Press
A Division of Thomas Nelson & Zondervan
1663 Liberty Drive
Bloomington, IN 47403
www.westbowpress.com
844-714-3454

New International Version (NIV)
Holy Bible, New International Version®, NIV® Copyright ©1973, 1978, 1984,
2011 by Biblica, Inc.® Used by permission. All rights reserved worldwide

ISBN: 979-8-3850-0694-6 (sc)
ISBN: 979-8-3850-0695-3 (e)

Library of Congress Control Number: 2023917116

Print information available on the last page.

WestBow Press rev. date: 09/18/2023

*I dedicate this book first and foremost to the **Lord** who gave Andy and me the story; to **our children** Clark, JB, Daniel, Philip, Ray and any others that God may give us; and to **teens** and **young singles** everywhere.*

"Seek the LORD while he may be found…"
Isaiah 55:6.

"Be joyful always; pray continually; give thanks in all circumstances, for this is God's will for you in Christ Jesus."
1 Thessalonians 5:16–18

CONTENTS

INTRODUCTION

> A cord of three strands is not quickly broken.
>
> —ECCLESIASTES 4:12

It seems fitting that I would start writing this story today because it was four years ago this week that I received a very special e-mail from a very special person. I was 28 years old. Here's what it said:

Hello Heather,

I am emailing you as someone you may or may not remember. I saw you at Oglebay [*a Young Life leader weekend*] and then your name came up in a conversation with Bob McGinnis. He told me a little about you and then I asked him for a contact. As for me, I live in Ohio just west of Wheeling. I've been involved in Young Life for a long time. I came to Christ through this ministry. Anyway, I would like to call you or get together sometime... maybe take in a movie. I'm guessing you may be at Rockbridge this weekend. I'll be praying for you.

Peace,
Andy Nelson <><
P.S. I'm under Bruce Andrew Nelson in Facebook

I could write that this one e-mail changed my life forever, but it's more than that. My life *has* been changed forever, and it started much earlier than 2007. I hope you'll read on to know a true-life love story involving three main characters. It started with One.

Chapter 1

I MET HIM

In the beginning was the Word...
and the Word was God

—JOHN 1:1

I am one of those people who loved most things about high school life. I was involved with student council, played on the soccer team, and had some really good friends (although never a *best* friend). I was involved with my church youth group and attended church most Sundays. Yet as much as I enjoyed life and school, I was an average teenage girl: I struggled with being a little overweight, I put pressure on myself to get good grades, and I was always hoping to be more popular. At home, my family owned a dairy farm and we were pretty close (my parents, older brother, Jed, younger sister, Meghan, and me). We knew the value of hard work, the importance of family, and the art of hospitality. In the big scheme of things, I had no significant worries, and I was content thinking about myself, my friends, and my family. *Was there more to life than this?*

In tenth grade I became closer friends with Robyn, Maria, and Lori (all on the soccer team with me) who kept talking about this group they were a part of called Campus Life (also known as Youth for Christ). I decided I would go to one of the weekly club meetings to see what it was about. It was a blast! It was like youth group only cooler, because everyone from our school was invited, and lots more kids came. At first the meetings were in a girl's house, but soon we outgrew the house and moved to the local community center. So many kids were coming to eat the snacks, play silly games, and have a discussion.

That fall (1994), Campus Life invited students to a weekend away in Salt Fork, Ohio. My friends were going, and I definitely didn't want to miss this chance to make more friends from other cities. The whole weekend was so much fun. Kids from all over the region came, and we played games, sang songs, watched funny skits, stayed up late, had great dinners, and talked a lot. There was a speaker who shared each day about Jesus…but it seemed different from what our church preacher shared. This speaker was talking directly to us kids in a way that we could relate to and understand. He became our friend and laughed and played games with us all weekend. We all listened when he shared his stories. Saturday night, he gave a message that spoke right to my heart.

The speaker shared that each of us is created with a God-shaped hole (so to speak) in our hearts. He said that many of us try to fill this hole (or void) with other things besides God. Some of us turn to boyfriends or girlfriends, drugs, alcohol, good grades, friends, popularity, and so on. But these things will never fit perfectly into that hole. I had never thought about this before. I realized I was one of those who tried to fill the God-shaped hole with things that would never fit or fill the void completely. Being popular and beautiful and getting good grades would never fill the void in my heart that only God could. The speaker also shared that believing in Jesus Christ as our Savior gives us a purpose and direction in life. The purpose is to love God and love others. The words of Jesus give us direction on how to live out this purpose.

As a teenage girl, I had never thought seriously about why we are on this earth and what my purpose was. But that day I believed in the love Jesus talked about. I believed He *was* the answer and could fill the void I had been striving to fill. I believed I needed to make a change in my life. And so it was on that day in November

1994 that I met Him. I met Jesus—my friend, my mentor, my hero, and my Savior. I asked Him to come into my heart and change me. I wanted Him to fill the void and give me a purpose greater than I had ever known. He did and He has.

Chapter 2

MATURING ME

Therefore, if anyone is in Christ, he is a new
creation; the old has gone the new has come.

—2 CORINTHIANS 5:17

I wish I could say after my trip to Salt Fork that life was perfect,
but instead it was a time of growing with both ups and downs.
I continued to be a part of Campus Life and attended everything
possible—clubs, fall retreats, summer camps, and Bible studies with
the leaders. I loved everything about it, and it made high school
that much more fun. I was also learning more in youth group. I
continued to work hard in school and did my best to love God and
love others. As far as boys went, I had some crushes on a few guys
in high school, but they never seemed to reciprocate. I was always
the *friend* and never the *girl*friend. I didn't really let it get me down,
though, and kept pretty busy with all the high school things. Like a
lot of girls, I hoped college would be the place I'd meet my match.

Moving away for college was a sweet time for me to grow in my
faith and Christian friendships. The Lord used those friendships
and the preaching at the campus church to mature me in my study
of the Word and get me excited about who Jesus was and is. I also
joined a small group and had an accountability partner who read
the New Testament with me and encouraged me in prayer. God was
also good to give me more than a handful of great male friends, but
I remained the *friend* and never the *girlfriend*.

I majored in Spanish education and graduated in May 2001 from

Virginia Tech (VT) but decided not to teach right away. I accepted a job with VT admissions instead; however, after a year away from teaching I felt strongly the Lord wanted me to return. In the summer of 2002, I moved back home and applied for Spanish teaching jobs in Pennsylvania. I was offered a job at Valley Middle School (VMS) just north of Pittsburgh and moved within the month of accepting it. The town was about one hour's drive away from my parents' house and very foreign to me. I had no friends or connections there. I had to trust the Lord.

Chapter 3

MY CALLING TO YOUNG LIFE

> Freely you have received, freely give.
>
> —MATTHEW 10:8

Moving to New Kensington, Pennsylvania, was a big step for me. It was a new city, a new apartment, and a new job. I knew the Lord would continue to protect me as I went to my first day of work—new teacher in-service. I connected with another new teacher, Michelle, and we hung out a few times. I shared with her that I felt the Lord calling me to volunteer with high school kids after school. She thought she was being called too.

In mid-September 2002, I looked in the telephone book (for the younger readers this was a book printed annually with names, numbers and addresses of people and places in the area) to see if there was a Christian ministry to teens where Michelle and I could volunteer. I knew of two that were common: Campus Life and Young Life (YL). Thankfully, there was a Young Life in the telephone book. I called them and they invited me to their first big event, *Thirty Foot Sundae*, to be held the following day. I really don't think they had any idea why I was calling or if I'd show up. I invited Michelle and we went together after school.

We arrived early, and after meeting the area director, Bob McGinnis, and his wife, Randi, we were put to work to help make the thirty-foot ice cream sundae. It would be the first of many events that I would spend getting to know high school kids in the Allegheny Valley. Michelle and I enjoyed our time with YL that fall and signed on with Allegheny Valley YL to be two of their volunteer leaders. It was a great fit for us. We instantly had new friends and sisters and brothers in the faith to spend time with in our new hometown. In addition to weekly YL club, we also met weekly for leadership meetings. Bob and Randi became our close friends along with their two daughters, Beth and Bobbi.

I fell in love with the ministry of Young Life almost instantly. It was leader-driven and a ministry focused on relationships. Leaders would spend time with kids and become their friends, sharing most everything with them. This then gave the leaders the opportunity to share the hope they have in Christ with their new friends. Besides the focus on relationships, the music, use of humor, and spiritual content of YL Clubs drew me in too. It seemed from that time on if I wasn't teaching, I was volunteering with high school kids and Young Life in my free time. I looked forward to it and loved being a part of something bigger than myself.

Chapter 4

ANDY

> But seek first his kingdom and his righteousness,
> and all these things will be given to you as well.
>
> **—MATTHEW 6:33**

On the other side of the Ohio River, Andy was also growing up and attending high school where the most important things to him were his family (parents and two younger brothers), sports (playing and watching), and fitting in with his peers. In ninth grade, Andy met a college student named Thomas Grey, better known as *Buc*. Buc befriended Andy and invited him to Young Life club. At first, Andy wasn't too impressed with Young Life club, but he came back occasionally to see his friend, Buc. He was also intrigued by Young Life summer camp. He knew he wanted to go because Buc wanted him to go and he didn't want to let him down.

In June 1995, buses left from Andy's hometown to head to Young Life Castaway Club camp in Minnesota. Andy was excited from the start. He really enjoyed all the adventure things to do at camp, as well as the program team, the food, living in a dorm with friends, and all the cool surprises at YL camp. Throughout the week there was a speaker who shared stories about Jesus's life. Toward the end of the week Andy heard one of the program speakers share his story (testimony). The man shared that he liked sports and his favorite athlete was Michael Jordan. He shared how he knew one day Michael Jordan was going to retire from sports and eventually *meet his Maker* (God). God would not ask Jordan how many points he scored playing basketball or how many titles he won. He would ask him something like 'Do you know me?'

The man went on to share that while man often looks at outward appearances, God looks at the heart. Andy recognized that he was basing his life on his performance and acceptance from others. In the end, it was all very selfish and had no eternal significance. Yet, a relationship with God had purpose. Andy believed these things and wanted to live out His purpose in life—to love God and give glory to Him. Andy's faith, as small as a mustard seed, started taking root that week.

Andy's new life was impacted most by some great men and women of the faith. After accepting Christ at camp, Andy joined a Bible study group called campaigners. Later, he would be a part of a young men's discipleship group that met weekly with some Young Life leaders. This helped grow Andy's faith as a follower of Jesus. The summer after graduating high school, Andy had a great opportunity to volunteer as a part of *work crew* at a Young Life camp in Virginia. Andy loved the fellowship of working together with other believers. He also learned about humility while working behind the scenes.

That fall Andy started college, and in December a friend asked him to attend a Campus Crusade for Christ conference in Indiana. It was there that the Lord put on Andy's heart to do more outreach with his faith. So with the start of the spring semester, he started volunteering at a local high school as a Young Life leader. In 2002 Andy completed his degree in history with a minor in business. He knew he wanted to work for Young Life after graduating, though, and he started his first, full time job as a YL intern later that year in Toronto, Ohio.

Chapter 5

FIRST SIGHTS

> But the Lord looks at the heart
>
> **—1 SAMUEL 16:7**

In the fall of 2002, Bob and Randi asked me to take some students to something called Young Life fall weekend in Erie, Pennsylvania. It was very similar to Campus Life's Salt Fork. I was excited to spend an entire weekend becoming a friend to the students and sharing with them about Jesus. I was also very nervous since it was my first *YL weekend*. I had no idea what to expect; however, at YL events it is common to have leadership meetings to inform the leaders what will happen each day.

It was at one of these meetings that Andy first saw me. He recalls seeing me laughing and smiling with some friends and thinking to himself how joyful a person I must be. (Years later he would share with me that he thought a person like me would be someone good to have in his life.) I was so distracted that weekend trying to figure out everything that I honestly don't remember seeing Andy. I do remember really enjoying my time with the kids.

It was not until January 2003 that I first put a name to a face with Andy Nelson. Bob and Randi had invited Michelle and me to attend the area's regional leader weekend at Oglebay Park in West Virginia. We were happy to have a weekend away with other YL leaders. Friday night we went into the conference room early and saw a few people there already. Beth had said that one of the program guys at the conference was named Andy Nelson from St.

Clairsville, Ohio. Michelle instantly piped up because her fiancé, Adam, was also from St. Clairsville. She went over to talk with Andy and introduced herself. It turns out that Andy and Michelle's fiancé were neighbors growing up. Andy knew Adam well and was happy to meet Michelle at a YL weekend.

I didn't think too much beyond that it was a neat coincidence that Michelle's fiancé knew Andy. From what I saw of Andy that weekend he seemed like a nice guy. I remember him having a thick beard and being thin. I also remember that he and a friend did some skits in front of everyone to entertain us. He did a good job and made everyone laugh. Also, each morning of the leader weekend a few leaders would come pray for their areas in a room near the conference hall. I volunteered to go and saw a handful of leaders there. Andy was there too. (It seemed he would always be one of the leaders there praying when I would attend future Oglebay leader weekends.)

Chapter 6

PREPARING ME

> Finish your outdoor work and
> get your fields ready.
>
> **—PROVERBS 24:27**

It would be a few more years before Andy and I would really connect. The Lord had many other things planned for me before bringing a man into my life. However, it was at this time in 2003 that I wrote down qualities I was hoping my future husband would have. I wrote it on cardstock and kept it in my Bible (see picture). I began to pray these and pray for him, his family, his friends, and his decisions. I wondered when the Lord would make my husband known to me or if I was called to be married at all. I also began reading many books about being a woman after God's heart, a future wife, and dating in hopes that I would be prepared if it happened. In the meantime, I was definitely enjoying what He had me doing while single.

I would go on to teach Spanish at VMS and volunteer with YL through the summer of 2004. As great as things were with YL and friendships, though, teaching at a middle school became very stressful and difficult. My coworkers were great, but I did not enjoy going to work each day. Some of the students I really cared about while others were very disrespectful and came from hard situations.

LOVE - OF FAMILY   FRUITS   LEADER FAITH, PRAYER, SCRIPTURE   LIKES MUSIC, SINGING
    FRIENDS   ATTRACTIVE - TO ME   LIKES TO TRAVEL
    KIDS   CREATIVE!   LOVES ME
JOY - FROM JESUS   ROMANTIC   FUNNY
    SMALL THINGS IN LIFE   SMART   RESPECT
PEACE - RELAXED   AMBITIOUS   TALLER THAN ME?
    NOT A WORRY WART   FAMILY - CENTERED   NICE SMILE
PATIENCE - WITH ME   DOESN'T GET EASILY DISGUSTED   NICE EYES
    MY IMPERFECTIONS   GOOD LISTENER, CONVERSATIONALIST   MUSCLES
    MY NEEDS + WANTS   OPEN-MINDED - OTHER CULTURES, LANGUAGES   NICE BACK MUSCLE
KINDNESS - ALL HUMANS   HEALTHY, BUT NOT TOO OBSESSIVELY/EXERCISE   NO FACIAL HAIR?
GOODNESS - CHARITY, POOR, WEAK   ENJOYS BOARD GAMES, CARDS, MOVIES
GENTLENESS - ANIMALS, MY ♥, PEOPLE   SUPPORTIVE
FAITHFULNESS - IN JESUS   NOT A DRINKER
    THE WORLD   LIKES DUES, SOCCER, FOOTBALL, HOCKEY   VT
    ME   TEACH ME NEW THINGS, ENCOURAGE ME TO RISK
    MARRIAGE   LIKES TO DANCE
SELF CONTROL - MONEY, HIS MOUTH   SMILES OFTEN
    FOOD
    HEALTH   5/27/03

In the spring of 2004, I felt it was time for a change. I thought teaching at the high school level would be better for me, yet I lacked confidence in my Spanish ability. Should I consider doing some more traveling and immerse myself in Spanish before applying for high school jobs? Time would tell. I resigned from my teaching job in June and made plans for bigger and better things.

In the fall of 2004 I travelled to San José, Costa Rica, where I lived and studied for five months. I also volunteered with Young Life there (called Vida Joven). I grew in my faith, as well as my Spanish. (I have many stories from that time in my life but that would be for another book.) At the end of January 2005, it was time for me to return home to the states. I had had a few dreams in Spanish and my fluency had improved tremendously. I felt the Lord was telling me to come home.

I returned in late January but didn't make it in time for the annual YL leader weekend at Oglebay… sadly. My parents were apprehensive about me not having a job to come home to, but I was happy about that. It would be a time to relax until schools had teacher openings in the fall. I decided I would knit and sell scarves to make some spare money if I couldn't find a full-time job. Seriously.

The Lord had other plans. I started attending my home church (Bethel Church) again, and soon my mom heard there was a Spanish teacher needed at our friend's school thirty-five minutes away—West Greene. I sent in a resume, had two interviews, and was hired. I started work within three weeks of being back in the states. Clearly the Lord wanted me to teach (and not knit). He provides!

Chapter 7

CONNECTING

And what does the Lord require of you?
To act justly and to love mercy and
to walk humbly with your God.

—MICAH 6:8

West Greene High School was a great fit for me. I loved teaching high school kids, and I loved how I could relate to them better—it being in a rural community (Valley was more like a city). My students were so fun, but they, too, were lost spiritually. I quickly realized there was not a lot of ministries for youth going on in the area. Youth groups were practically nonexistent at the small churches, and most kids didn't attend church.

I asked the Lord to show me where to do outreach. I met with a man named Chris Buda (YL River Region Director) about what it might look like to start a Young Life club at West Greene. He later connected me with John Aderholt in Morgantown, West Virginia. Wouldn't you know that the Mountaineer Area YL in Morgantown had been praying for schools in Fayette and Greene Counties, Pennsylvania, for the past few years? I began to meet with community folks and search for future leaders to reach kids with me. It was an amazing time of seeing the Lord work in relationships. By fall of 2006, we had some things going with YL in Greene County, and the leadership consisted of a few Waynesburg University students and myself.

In January 2007 a few new leaders and I geared up to go to the YL regional weekend at Oglebay Park. John Aderholt included us in all aspects of his area's team and led our time there. I was pretty busy talking with adults and Greene County leaders, but I made time to go to the morning prayer gatherings where I saw many leaders, including Andy. I remember walking by him in the hallway at one point and saying, "hey", casually.

Andy also remembers seeing me. He remembers at one point during the worship he sat down to pray. Somebody behind him put their hand on his shoulder. Andy ignored it at the time. Later, he turned back to acknowledge his neighbor as if to say, "thanks for your concern, I'm ok." Yet the people behind didn't pay attention to him. He looked around wondering who touched him, and across the room he saw me. He didn't know my name, only a face he had seen before.

A few weeks passed and Andy (while working for YL fulltime) had a regional staff meeting at Chris Buda's house. At some point during the day, he joined in on a conversation with Bob McGinnis and John Aderholt talking about a girl leader that was really amazing and doing good things for Young Life. John turned to Andy and said, "you guys would be perfect together." Andy pondered these things and would later e-mail Bob to find out my full name and contact information:

> Hey McGinnis,
>
> I'm emailing you because yesterday you sparked my curiosity when speaking of Heather Gracie. I noticed a pretty red head at Oglebay and wondered if this is the girl you were speaking of. If so, I'd like to call her or meet up with her sometime. Do you have a contact? Let me know.
>
> Thanks,
> Nelson

Bob responded:

Andy,

Actually glad to hear this. Her name is Heather Grice and her email is …

McGinnis

On February 24, 2007, Andy sent me the e-mail that I've included in the beginning of this book (see Introduction). It arrived in my junk e-mail box but I was able to catch it. I was surprised to receive an e-mail from Andy who was someone I hardly knew. Upon reading that Bob had given him my information, I figured Bob must have been playing matchmaker. I was not that excited to go out with Andy, somewhat of a stranger, but I had decided earlier that year that I would date any guy once. (It was what all those dating books had said.) Andy had given me his info to look him up on Facebook, so I did and he seemed like a good guy. I replied:

Andy,

Oooohh Bob McGinnis...that man just can't stop talking about me! Haha! Yes, Andy, I remember you...and to be honest on the first 'meet-up' I'd prefer to do a lunch or ice cream or something rather than a movie...especially since I don't know you all that well...and who likes talking during movies?

Are you doing YL full time? If you are, I'm sure you're as busy or busier than I am trying to start YL down here in Greene County, PA. I might be able to swing something this Saturday, but next weekend we're doing a work weekend at Lake Champion so I'll be out of town. Weekdays are equally unfriendly it's sad to say...

Thanks for praying for us this past weekend, but we actually weren't at Rockbridge (we don't have a campaigners/club yet...still just trying to do contact work/grow leaders). We'll take any prayers we can get though.

I will add you to my Facebook...My name is Heather Grice.

Blessings,
Heather

He agreed and we exchanged phone numbers to coordinate. I remember hearing his voice on the phone for the first time and what a great voice it was... masculine, kind, friendly. We would talk a few more times before deciding to meet on a Saturday afternoon in March at a Cabela's store in Wheeling, West Virginia. (This would become a central location for us being that Andy lived in Belmont County, Ohio, and I was living in a double-wide trailer at the family farm in Washington.)

It was a little cool in early March, so I chose to wear jeans, a form-fitting maroon sweater, brown dressy boots with a heel, and a coat. I tried to look my best but wasn't getting my hopes up since I didn't really know this guy. I was still nervous though. I arrived on time and met Andy at the entrance to Cabela's. As I walked toward him, I saw he was wearing an Ohio State jacket, Ohio State hat, and Ohio State polo shirt. I guessed he liked Ohio State☺. We shook hands and started our walk inside Cabela's.

I don't remember much of that conversation, but I do remember we talked a lot and I'm certain we were both a little nervous. After walking around Cabela's for a bit and seeing the 'dead zoo', as I call it, we decided to grab lunch at a nearby Applebee's restaurant. At lunch I think we both felt more comfortable. I remember he talked about his brothers, his family, YL, substitute teaching, and his favorite teams. We had a lot in common. He asked me questions about my family, YL, Virginia Tech, and my job. He was a good listener, and I knew we would be great friends. He paid for our meal and held the doors for me (a perfect gentleman). We walked back toward our cars in the huge Cabela's parking lot. Andy mentioned he had an appointment at 3:30PM but was free until then if I wanted to go for a drive around Wheeling. I didn't have anything else to do, and I was enjoying our conversation, so I agreed.

As we walked in the parking lot, he pointed out his car; a 1997 Honda Civic Sedan. Unknowingly, I had parked three cars down—a 2005 Honda Civic Sedan. I could not believe A) he drove the same type of car as me B) I parked in the same row as him and C) his car was a stick shift like mine. Maybe I had made the right decision to hang out more with this guy. I got in the car and noticed it was not super clean on the inside (I would journal that night that his car *had seen better days*). I liked Andy more. (I had been around a handful of guys previously that cared about their cars more than people and kept them immaculate. I had hoped my future guy would not be like one of those guys.) As Andy started to drive toward Wheeling, he then told me about his 3:30PM appointment. It was to have his car fixed for making noises while going around turns. They were some funny sounds to hear as we drove over to Wheeling Park and went in and out of curves and up and down hills.

On the way out of Wheeling he took me to his old YL office in a small, Episcopalian church. Although he no longer had an office there, he still had the key. I felt a little leery going inside an empty church with a guy I just met and looking around without permission, but Andy seemed excited to tell me all about it. It was fun spending time together.

He dropped me off at my car and I said something silly like 'hope the car appointment goes well,' as we parted. As he drove away, I was mad at myself for not saying, 'thank you,' and that, 'I had a fun time.' I did hope he'd call me to go out again.

Within the hour after parting, I received a phone call. I was surprised when I saw it was Andy. I said "hello" and he seemed just as surprised that he called me as I was to hear from him. He truthfully didn't mean to call me. However, because he did, I was able to thank him for the date and lunch. I also gave him the go-ahead to call me again some time. I was so thankful that he accidentally called so I could tell him all that.

We both had such busy lives ahead of us that I wondered when we would be able to meet again. The following weeks we e-mailed and called a few times. I remember especially feeling touched though when Andy sent me a text message, "Good luck tonight," for our Mr. West Greene competition that I sponsored. I didn't even have texting on my cell phone plan at the time. I didn't care—I was so impressed he remembered the event when we had just met two weeks prior. We really hadn't talked about it that much either. Wow! This was a guy I should get to know more.

Our second date went just as well. We spent an afternoon walking around Oglebay Park (yup, the same one where the YL leader weekend was held annually). Then we went for ice cream. I liked Andy more but was still unsure where this was leading since we were both so busy. He also told me he was planning to go to China in May for a two-week YL mission trip with Chris Buda.

The third time we would see each other was when I invited him to come to a party at my house. Some friends from my small group were coming over to play volleyball and games. We thought it might be a good chance for Andy to invite some of his friends, too, so we could get to know each other in a group setting. I was nervous for him to meet some of my friends and see my house. I was glad to have good friends there to put me at ease. Andy arrived with his brother, Luke, and his friend, Josh. Andy and Luke were so good at volleyball. I was impressed more. We had fun playing all the games and visiting with each other's friends. It was a good night. I wasn't sure if I'd see him again before he took his two-week-trip to China so I hugged him goodbye and hoped we'd keep in touch by phone or e-mail in the meanwhile.

We did talk on the phone a few more times before he went to China in May. I remember texting him Matthew 28:19 as he headed off—*Therefore go and make disciples of all nations, baptizing them in the name of the Father and of the Son and of the Holy Spirit.*

My birthday was while he was away—May 19th. The day came and went and nothing from Andy…but I told myself to be okay with it since he was in a completely different country.

Chapter 8

A TIME FOR EVERYTHING

Go to the land I will show you.

—GENESIS 12:1

Andy returned in early June, and we spoke on the phone briefly about his trip. He said he felt the Lord was calling him to go to China long term as a teacher starting in August. I didn't know what to think. I was a little shocked and wondered what he was thinking about our future relationship during his teaching time away in China.

Both of us became very busy and the phone conversations were less frequent and shorter. By mid-June I felt like something was different. I finally told Andy I wanted to talk about it, and we both shared our thoughts on the phone. It was a little difficult to discuss, but we decided to just be friends while he was heading to China in the fall. I was okay with it, though a little bummed. I did still want to meet one more time to give him things he had left at the party. I also wanted to say goodbye and wish him well in China. He agreed to meet me at the Ohio Valley Mall that Friday.

I drove out to the mall awaiting a phone call from Andy of when he'd be free to come meet me. I shopped and waited...and waited. Eventually, I called and asked if he was able to come. He was still at the camp but said he'd come meet me if I was okay to wait a little longer for him to get there. *Had he forgotten that I was coming?* I waited.

Finally, he met me and we went to a Denny's restaurant to have dinner. It was good to see him again. I remember he looked so cute that day. He wore a blue t-shirt that made his nice green eyes stick out and he had recently shaved his beard. I asked lots of questions about China and what was new since we parted last. He talked a lot about his camp job as well and some struggles he was having there. I listened. He didn't ask me too many questions, which I thought was strange, but it made the goodbye a little easier.

The meal ended casually—like two friends. I paid for my meal and he paid for his. I gave him some brownies I had made, and we hugged goodbye. I said I'd be in touch via e-mail while he was in China. I was okay to be friends, thinking anything more would probably never happen.

Chapter 9

E-MAILS

Let us encourage one another

—HEBREWS 10:25

Andy was off to China in late August, and I was back at West Greene teaching Spanish and leading YL in my free time. I had kept pretty busy the rest of the summer and tried not to think too much about what might have been with Andy Nelson. I definitely considered him a good friend—so much that I remember calling him the day my first niece, Elsie, was born in August 2007. He was excited for our family. I was glad to hear his voice again.

After he had gone to China, I e-mailed him a couple times a month with a hello or info about some college football games, YL, or fun things about the family. He would respond in kind. In October I got on Facebook to look him up and see if he had any recent updates from his time in China. To my surprise, his profile was not posted anymore. I thought I would send him an e-mail to make sure he was still okay:

Andy,

It looks like your Facebook acct is no more...Did you delete it? Is everything okay? I hope China is treating you well this week.

Stuff here is busy as usual. You know how it goes. College football has been pretty exciting these past few weeks. I hope you've been able to catch a few games. It was sweet seeing USC lose yesterday.

Peace,
Heather
"Be **joyful always**." 1 Thess. 5:16
"**Faithfulness** is our responsibility; **results are God's**." K Shafer

Wouldn't you know that this small e-mail of concern on my part would set Andy's mind to prayerfully think more about us being together. I was unaware of these thoughts he was having. I only knew that I liked having an e-mail buddy in China. We would e-mail more frequently after this but I was still very unaware of his thoughts and feelings.

On December 25th I returned to my house after a full day of Christmas fun with our new niece, Elsie, and the family. I had left my cell phone at the house all day. I had some text messages and a couple voicemails when I got home. One voicemail was from Andy saying Merry Christmas and that he hoped all was well. I was excited, but more surprised than anything. This was the first real time I remember thinking that Andy must like me for more than just an e-mail buddy. He called me on Christmas!? Who does that unless they really care for someone?

For him, the spark was an e-mail. For me, it was a voicemail on Christmas. I began to pray more about Andy's and my future after this message wondering what he was thinking and if this was from the Lord. I also shared this with my family and my accountability partner, Melanie, at the time. They were all very encouraging in how to proceed and what to say and do next. They agreed that it seemed like I had someone pursuing me.

Considering how much I've always loved e-mails, and e-mailing, and letter-writing, I was delighted to see what would happen next, but I guarded my heart and proceeded with caution. After all it was December and he was living in China. I would not be seeing him face to face again until he would be home in July.

Chapter 10
RETURN FROM CHINA

Trust in the LORD with all your heart.
—PROVERBS 3:5

In January 2008 I received my first mailed letter from China. It was brief but to the point. Andy said he'd like to spend more time with me in the summer when he got home. I sent him an e-mail saying I had received it, and from that time on a steady flow of e-mails and letters were sent back and forth from China to the states. We kept our snail mail letters more fun, and light, while via e-mail we would ask questions to get to know each other better.

Andy felt strongly we should keep our focus on Christ while pursuing each other long distance. He was good to communicate with me regarding e-mailing and letter writing boundaries so we wouldn't become obsessed. This was good for me because I had become pretty fixated on checking my e-mail and mailbox on a daily (sometimes hourly) basis.

Andy arrived home after his first year in China on July 2, 2008. We were both anxious and nervous and wondering what the summer would hold for us after parting ways in June 2007. I never would've guessed after our meeting in June that we would be hanging out again over a year later. I had thought it was done—that just a friendship was in store. God obviously had other plans.

We decided to meet for breakfast on July 4th at the Cracker Barrel restaurant near my hometown. We hugged. It was a new feeling being with him and having him in the same country after only phone calls and letters the past few months. We both ate well and were still nervous, but the conversation was natural.

The big thing I remember him sharing was in regards to his future career. He didn't know much but said he knew he was called to return to China for one more year of teaching before coming back to the US. He also felt God leading him to ministry down the road but was not sure in what capacity. Maybe with Young Life staff? Maybe an international ministry? Maybe China? He did say he didn't think it was to be a pastor. I listened and tried not to show my inward thoughts of being surprised and shocked.

Would God really lead me to a guy that might be a missionary in another country? Or to China? Was that to be my future? I studied Spanish not Chinese. Selfishly I thought about how I liked my comfort zone in the states where I knew people and was near my family. Plus, I was enjoying my job and YL was going well in Greene County. Was I really being called to leave all that? I knew God was asking me for faithfulness.

When we parted that Independence Day morning, I believe we made plans to hang out soon. I thought about that conversation for many days and began to pray and seek counsel. I e-mailed my friend and elder sister in Christ, Boo Andrews, who shared a similar experience she had had and also pointed me to Ephesians 3:20-21, *Now to him who is able to do **immeasurably more than all we ask or imagine**, according to his power that is at work within us, to him be glory in the church and in Christ Jesus throughout all generations, forever and ever! Amen.*

What a gift God's Word is. Why was I being anxious about what Andy had shared? If it's the Lord's will for me to be with Andy, then I need to be faithful and obedient and excited. The Lord has big plans and blessings for me, and they are immeasurably more than I could ask or imagine. Once God showed me this, I began to get more comfortable with whatever His plan might be. I would try my best to trust Him.

Chapter 11

MEETING PARENTS AND FRIENDS

Honor your father and mother...

—EXODUS 20:12

Looking back, I can see how meeting each other's families may have been too much too soon for our friendship. However, timeliness was in order since Andy would be going back to China again in late August.

I wanted desperately for my sister and her family to meet Andy and give me their feedback. They would be leaving for their home in Maryland on a Sunday afternoon following the holiday weekend at the farm. We pushed to have lunch before they left and decided we would invite Mom and Dad as well. Andy was on board and we (my sister, Meghan, her husband, Jace, their daughter, Elsie, Mom and Dad and I) planned to meet Andy for lunch at Cheddar's restaurant in Wheeling. I drove separately and met Andy first.

I remember it was a warm day, and I chose to wear a skirt. Andy said I looked nice (or something to that extent). I was flattered. I prepped him a little and asked if he would do me a favor if he felt comfortable with it—would he ask to say a blessing before we ate? (My family was not in the habit of doing this.) He agreed. I cannot imagine what he may have been feeling or thinking at this moment (awaiting my family), but I am certain if I was in his shoes (meeting a gal's dad for the first time), I would have had lots of butterflies in my stomach and probably would have felt sick. Andy seemed somewhat relaxed.

Andy and I were seated at a side booth, and we patiently awaited the arrival of everyone. I believe Andy met Mom first, then Dad, shaking hands with both. Then Meghan (while holding a sleeping Elsie) gave Andy a hug and finally, Jace shook his hand. We sat down and got Elsie situated. I sat across from Andy. Dad was his normal chatty self when meeting new people. We talked about random things—mostly about China and farming—but it seemed to go well. When the food arrived Andy remembered about the blessing. Everyone agreed to bow their heads. I was inwardly overjoyed.

Since Dad and Elsie had never been to the *dead zoo* in Cabela's, we decided we should all take a tour since it was nearby. (This was where Andy and I spent our first date if you remember.) At Cabela's, Dad talked more with Andy while we entertained Elsie running ahead. Meghan took some pictures of the whole event. It was a fun afternoon. My family returned to the farm after while Andy and I drove on to St. Clairsville to meet his parents in Ohio.

Andy had a few things planned before stopping to meet his mom at the Jamboree in the Hills' office. (Jamboree in the Hills was an annual country concert held in the Ohio Valley.) He showed me Ohio University Eastern campus where he had attended, and we walked a path with a red covered bridge and picked some berries. I wasn't sure what he was thinking about walking and visiting such a romantic spot, but I was nervous and hoped we could just keep talking and get to know one another amidst some beautiful scenery. We did just that, and it was great.

Meeting Donna Nelson, Andy's mom, was a lot of fun. I wasn't really nervous because I love people, and meeting *new* people is fun for me. She gave me a big hug and must have held me in the hug for a good two minutes or so. (It seemed like a long time, but maybe it wasn't two minutes.) She was so excited to finally meet me after all that Andy had shared. I also met her good friend, Shelly, and they were both so joyful and pleasant. I loved them instantly. Andy borrowed a golf cart and showed me around the Hills' property which was pretty cool. When we got back, we offered to help Donna and Shelly with some mailings. I was happy to serve alongside Andy, and we were able to talk more too, so that was good. I remember being really impressed because it was while we were working that Andy shared how he remembered seeing me for the first time at Young Life fall weekend in 2002. *Oh my! Six years ago!?* That fall weekend was a complete blur for me being my first YL experience and all, but for him to notice me was encouraging. *Who was this guy?* I don't consider myself to be the type of gal that gets noticed. He followed up by sharing how he remembers seeing me later that summer at Michelle (my teacher friend in New Kensington) and Adam's wedding in June, too. Wow!

That evening we also stopped at Andy's parents' house to meet his dad, Bruce Nelson. What a sweet guy! He seemed so jolly amidst dealing with Multiple Sclerosis on a daily basis. I was impressed to say the least. He seemed excited to meet me. Andy threw together some dinner that Donna had left in the refrigerator for us, and it was yummy. As Andy said the blessing, he thanked God for being able to spend time with me. What a sweetheart. I remember doing lots of the talking as Bruce continued to ask me questions about myself, VT, YL, the farm, etc. It was good. The most memorable part of the conversation was when Bruce said how much he had always loved the name 'Heather.' *Really? I don't even like my name all that much.* At first, I said something silly like, "you probably tell all of the girlfriends that." He said he didn't know why, but, truthfully, he's always liked it and thought it was such a great name. He even wanted his youngest sister to have the name Heather or Jessica. (Her name is Holly). Wild, huh? I felt like it was a mini-sign pointing me to the Nelson family.

Andy took me for a walk in his neighborhood after dinner then on a mini-tour of their house and all the Longaberger baskets (his mom sells them), the Ohio State Buckeye room, etc. It was a very nice home.

Andy later drove me back to my car in Wheeling. When we stopped, he reached in his pocket to give me a little souvenir from China. I had no idea what it might be. He said it was just something small. When he handed me a magnet in the shape of China, my heart leapt with joy. How did Andy remember that I collected magnets from other cities and countries? Wow! I think I may have told him about it briefly over a year prior, but never in my wildest dreams did I expect him to remember this. This was a special guy. We hugged goodbye and got a quick picture. It was a great day. We had survived each other's families and had thoroughly enjoyed each other's company. What a praise!

I returned home that night and already had an e-mail awaiting me, "Heather, you're amazing...Thanks for a great day...see you soon! – Andy"

TRIP TO DC

Within a week of being back in the states, Andy asked me if I'd accompany him to Washington DC to visit some friends. This would be our first road trip together. We would be driving about six hours, spending two nights with his friends, then driving back home on a Sunday afternoon. I was definitely nervous, because I was still very unsure of our relationship, but I agreed.

At the first rest stop in Maryland, we took a walk and Andy asked if we could read something in the Bible together. He pointed me to 1 Corinthians 7. The title for the chapter said 'Marriage.' I started to feel anxious. We read it silently to ourselves at first and when I came across the parts that talked about "the wife's body does not belong to her alone but also to her husband," and "it is better to marry than to burn with passion," I became more nervous and was wondering why Andy wanted to read all this that day?

When we began to talk about the passage, I tried to speak

around those topics by bringing up other ideas from the chapter. These topics didn't last too long before Andy came right out and said what he was thinking. I don't remember the specifics, because I was so nervous, but he remembers sharing that he felt called to marriage and called to me. He also pointed out verse 28 that says "…but those who marry will face many troubles in this life…" I remember him saying that marriage would not be easy. I was very unsure how to respond, but Andy definitely sensed I was nervous.

I had no idea if Andy was to be my future husband, but I knew I wanted to keep spending time with him to find out. I was also jealous that he felt the Lord calling him to marriage with me, and I wasn't sure at all. *How was Andy so certain?* I thought the whole scenario of reading 1 Corinthians 7 together was a little awkward, but I tried to have a good attitude about it since we still had the whole road trip remaining. Little did I know this conversation would consume my thoughts the rest of the trip.

Traveling in DC and meeting Andy's friends was good, although at times I felt a little uneasy. Being with Andy's friends when Andy and I weren't really boyfriend and girlfriend seemed odd. I was wondering what his friends were thinking of me …and us. My stomach was in knots, and my head was full of thoughts on what to do the rest of the weekend. I guess I felt pressure that Andy wanted more of a commitment than I could give him at the moment. I didn't let these feelings ruin our time with his friends, however. We toured DC and Arlington and went to a Nationals' baseball game that night. It was really great. That evening I shared my thoughts with the girl I was staying with, Jen (who I had just met a few hours prior). She understood where I was coming from but encouraged me to see where things would go with Andy since he was a great Christian guy. She told me I should talk to him and tell him what I was thinking.

The next day I spent lots of brainpower thinking through exactly what I wanted to say to Andy or if I would say anything. I was praying the Lord would give us the right timing. The second evening we changed plans and drove to Baltimore to see my sister and her husband, Meghan and Jace, and spent the night before coming home on Sunday afternoon. I was pleased that Andy was okay to do this since I was more comfortable in my sister's house than with strangers. That evening the four of us played Scrabble (one of my favorite games). Even though I knew Andy didn't know too much about board games, he was a good sport and was happy to play. The best part was that he did so well but wasn't boastful. I liked this part of Andy— his humility. I also liked that he got along well with Meghan and Jace. This was good to see.

The ride home from Maryland started out slowly. I knew I needed to talk to Andy and share my feelings, but I didn't think I should do it while he was driving. We kept up with small talk until we again stopped at the Sideling Hill rest stop in Maryland. I asked Andy if we could sit and talk. Finally, I shared my heart with him. I told him I wasn't sure what the Lord was saying to me concerning the two of us being together since he was going back to China again in August and would be gone for another ten months. I told him I just wasn't as certain as he was. I needed more time with him.

He took it pretty well, considering I think I crushed his hopes of us being a couple sooner. I felt like a huge weight had been lifted off my shoulders as I had been thinking about the words to share for the past two days. We prayed and thanked God for His plan and our fun weekend with friends and family.

During the drive home we got to talking about baseball, football, and some things we liked and disliked as well as hopes for the future. It was natural conversation between friends, and I remember laughing a lot. We were becoming close friends, and I felt free to do that without added pressure. We had discussed the idea of not spending time with our parents again just yet, but that didn't last long. Within the hour my mom called and asked if we wanted to stop for dinner. We did and it was sweet to eat, just the four of us. I really started to like Andy more after the conversation at the rest stop where I shared my feelings. I think part of it was because we had both communicated our hearts with each other. Another part of it was I felt back in control again (maybe not a good thing?). The beginning of the road trip was somewhat of a low in my mind, but it ended on such a high that I was excited to hang out again soon.

A few days later Andy came over, and I made him dinner—lasagna. He enjoyed it and was grateful. Afterward we talked about what we could do on such a warm summer evening. He brought up the idea of playing basketball. I knew it was something he really enjoyed (even though I knew I was terrible at it). I gave in and recommended a nearby park. We had a good time, and an evening spent playing was especially good for Andy's heart. I noticed how great he was at the game and encouraged him a lot. He was patient with me in how pathetic I was (although I think I improved with some of his pointers). By the end, Andy had a foot blister from the flip-flops he was wearing, but he didn't care—he was enjoying the time playing together.

Chapter 12

INTIMATE FRIENDS?

> ...what God's will is—his good,
> pleasing, and perfect will.
>
> **—ROMANS 12:2**

We met up more throughout the rest of the summer, and one of our dates included a trip to Books-a-Million. We searched for a book with two copies so we could read together while we were apart. Choosing God's Best by Dr. Don Raunikar was just the book. As you know from reading this story so far, neither Andy nor I really dated previously. We wanted to get some counsel and help so we would be able to glorify God with our dating. It was a great idea to read together.

The book challenged us to give glory to God in all aspects of life including our dates. I definitely recommend this book. At first it speaks to the dating world. Then it gets into what it looks like to be in a Godly dating relationship. I was immediately intrigued and went to work doing lots of underlining in the book as I read and learned new things. Andy read his too, and we would come together to discuss the chapters—always good conversations. The book was an encouragement to us and pointed out some things we hadn't thought of before.

I read most of the book in late July when I was travelling to Costa Rica and Panama to visit friends. On the return flight I was seated next to the window and began to read. An older gentleman came and sat in the seat next to me. I noticed he had what looked like a Bible in his hand. It didn't take me long to ask if he was a Christian. The remainder of the flight was spent talking to him about many things: family, faith, relationships, travel, football, and so on. I even talked to him about the book and about Andy. He was a good guy and, like so many others, encouraged me in my relationship with Andy. He was excited for us and the story God was writing between us. At one point during that flight there was some of the worst turbulence I've ever experienced. I asked my new friend, Greg, if we could pray. He agreed and we did. The Lord was so evident in that flight by putting us next to each other and also by calming the storm (turbulence). Greg had just shared the story of Jesus calming the storm before the turbulence began. I am grateful for the many storms the Lord has calmed in my life as well as the ones in my heart.

At the conclusion of the summer, it was time for Andy and me to part ways again. Andy was headed to training, then China for his second year of teaching English. We had discussed our relationship off and on throughout the summer. I was so unsure what we could be if he was going to be gone again for almost a year. The last time I saw him was in my parents' driveway as we said goodbye. I had prepared a care package for him that included some clothes, candies, and a small journal of our summer memories with some verses. I told him it was his Christmas and birthday presents. We hugged goodbye. I was a little sad but knew we would still have phone calls a few more days before he flew to China.

I believe it was the same night or maybe the following night that I received a phone call from Andy. In a roundabout way he was asking me again where we stood in our relationship. "Were we boyfriend and girlfriend? Would I consider us intimate friends?" [1] Ten months apart was a long time. I didn't want to fully commit for fear of Andy meeting someone else in China, or for the possibility

---

[1] In the <u>Choosing God's Best</u> book it defines *Intimate friendship* as couples who have more intimate spiritual talks, share innermost thoughts, fears, failures, and hopes and minor physical touch like hand-holding/hugs.

of me meeting someone in America that sweeps me off my feet. I let Andy know I did not think we needed to consider ourselves boyfriend and girlfriend while he was in China. I was not ready for that. Looking back, I think it once again dampened Andy's spirit a bit and reminded him of the time he opened up to me at the Maryland rest stop a few weeks prior. He was so confident in the Lord's plan for the two of us, yet I was so guarded and unsure. Andy was zero for two in asking me to commit to him. He continued to persevere however, trusting in the Lord's leading.

Chapter 13

PACKAGES FROM AN UNKNOWN SENDER

Every good and perfect gift is from
above, coming down from the Father

—JAMES 1:17

The first weeks with Andy back in China were okay. I was connected with someone I could call *my guy*, yet not fully committed in case I would meet someone else. I liked where we were, and I had definitely underestimated the fun that Andy's return could be in regards to letter writing and letter receiving. One week after Andy had gone, I received a letter in the mail from him. (Most letters from China took two weeks to arrive). This envelope was in Andy's writing, but came from his home address in Ohio. I was impressed! He had left a letter for someone in his family to mail to me.

It didn't stop there. For the next three months I would periodically receive letters or packages from Andy, but not from China. All of them were written in his handwriting and prepared in advance to his departure. All of them arrived in perfect timing—when I was longing to hear from him and wondering about our friendship. One of the coolest packages sent was the book, The Heavenly Man by Brother Yun. Andy had read this book in preparation for being a missionary in China. He was now giving it to me with a note inside that warned me of the gravity of its contents. I began to read it that night and was blown away with this amazing story of a Christian brother's life in China. It is one of my favorite books to date.

It was soon after reading this book and receiving a few letters that I decided I should travel to China myself. If Andy would one day be called to live in China and I was to be his wife, I wanted to know I could live in the Chinese culture. A mutual friend of ours was also serving as a missionary teacher so I wanted to visit and encourage her as well. Win-win!

Chapter 14

I GO TO CHINA

I will be exalted among the nations

—PSALM 46:10

I had to jump through some hoops with my job to allow me time off to visit Andy in China, but it worked out. It was finally time for me to pack up and go. Christmas came and went. Thankfully, for the next part of the story I have both Andy's thoughts from his journal (in *italics*) and my thoughts (in **bold**) recorded to give you a greater sense of the whole trip.

DEC 24, 2008

It's Christmas Eve here in China. I'm excited for the gifts I have for my friends. Also, I'm thinking of the twelve days of gifts I have for Heather. I feel good about the gifts I am giving except the socks I have prepared for day six, isn't that what mothers give to their children? Oh well, that's just what I feel like giving. I know I want to give her flowers on day eight. The flowers must be red as the Chinese name I want to give her is "Hong Hua" or "Red Flower." Also, eight is a lucky number (in China) and I feel lucky to spend time with Heather. I hope this isn't too much too soon. I hope she will receive them. On day ten I want to give her ten pieces of chocolate, but I don't know what kind of chocolate she likes…dark, white, milk, with nuts, crispy rice? I want this to be perfect yet the real perfect gift has already been given to Heather in Jesus our Immanuel! ☺

DECEMBER 25, 2008

Today I awoke in the apartment of my friend Tim Corbin. He asked if I wanted to go running. "Sure", I said. And off we went. Tim and I run at a different pace and he said I could go ahead. I thought, "Well, he is wearing his MP3 and therefore not much for conversation so here goes nothing." I veered toward the sea and was in awe of the sun that was just above the horizon and reflecting off the sea. "I feel at peace in 'His' presence" I thought. And isn't that what He came to the earth to do…to bring hope and peace to mankind and salvation to those who will believe in His name! Also, I thought about Heather and how I wanted her to see this sunrise also…that we would witness His warmth and light and know that He is love.

Today Andy left me a voicemail wishing me a Merry Christmas. It reminded me of last year when I received a voicemail/phone call from him for the first time ever. I remember being extremely surprised that he had called last year because up to that point we had just e-mailed. It was that phone call that had me start praying more about a future with Andy. Now a year has passed and we are still in touch and prayerful about the future.

DECEMBER 27, 2008

So, I've prepared "twelve days of Christmas" for Heather. This is day two. Luke and Levi [Andy's brothers] *have been told to deliver encouraging text messages to Heather. I remember how Heather seemed to appreciate the text I sent her prior to the Mr. West Greene pageant in 2007. It's awesome how much she gives to the kids at WGHS.*

I packed all my bags up today and feel pretty good about it. I fit most all of *my* stuff in carry-ons and squeezed the gifts for Andy and others into the bigger, checked bags. They are soooo full!

DECEMBER 28, 2008

Today was the Clarke (my mom's family) Christmas and we all went to my Aunt Patty's. I was able to relax some since I was already packed up. I knew I would want to sleep some on the flight so I didn't go to bed until around 1AM.

DECEMBER 29, 2008

I'm so excited to see Heather! I feel that things are organized for Heather's stay except for this first day. I want to be ready and yet I don't feel ready. I don't even have the pick-up organized. Aahhh!! Lord, help!!

I can't believe I'm going to China!? What Spanish teacher does this?

Andy woke me up at 6:30AM today. He forgot the time change! My alarm was set for 7:30AM. He was excited and told me he and Jordan (Jo) would be there at the airport to meet me. Mom dropped me off at the Pittsburgh airport and I checked my luggage…with an odd feeling in the back of my mind that they probably wouldn't arrive with me. It was weird. I later realized in JFK airport that Delta never gave me baggage claim numbers! AAHH! I knew something was up. I tried to call Delta twice to no avail. I was only put on hold. I called Meghan [my sister] before boarding the flight to China and she took down all the info for me just in case. I prayed it would arrive with me, but I knew this would've been a miracle.

DECEMBER 30, 2008

After changing plans several times, I leave Qinhuangdao [my Chinese hometown] *by bus at noon to meet Jo (my Chinese friend) at the Beijing airport to welcome Heather. We watch the electric board and notice that Heather's plane arrived. Ninety minutes later I felt that she was ok, but I didn't know why it was taking this long. I started to pace. Should I go to the gift shop and buy her a flower? Was her luggage missing? Did I give her bad directions? Is she trying to call me? … Well, her luggage was lost and that turned out to be providential.*

What a pleasant memory I now have of seeing Heather walking towards me at the Beijing airport after months of separation. I was a little nervous and didn't know what to say. How could I not know what to say? I had months of anticipation. I suddenly felt clumsy. Walking became a challenge. To my delight, we decided to sit down in the airport and talk to Jo. I told Heather the Chinese name I picked out for her. Jo wasn't a big fan of the name, but Heather thought it was good and we went with it. Later, Heather and I boarded a charter bus for Qinhuangdao. We engaged in mostly small talk. I was nervous. On this ride Heather gave me a buckeyes' desk calendar which plays the OSU fight song! Does she know that I go on YouTube just to listen to the OSU Band? She's amazing!

After more than three hours on the bus, we arrived at Brad and Carrie Vaughn's (friends of mine) around midnight. I felt important to have a key to their apartment. However, the key didn't work. We knocked on the door until we woke them up and then I introduced the Vaughn's to Heather. They went back to bed. I gave Heather her stocking. She liked it. I liked that she liked it. I walked home feeling good.

The flights were smooth and I didn't have any problems entertaining myself. I talked with my neighbors, ate, slept, journaled, prayed, read and daydreamed. It was painless. I arrived in Beijing at 6:30PM. Surprisingly, the airport was

empty and quiet. Was this really one of the most populated cities in the world? At the baggage terminal I waited and waited... NOTHING! My bags never came! Because of what happened earlier I was not shocked. I saw a handful of people go to the Air China Lost and Found (thankfully written in English). I waited in line for maybe twenty minutes before speaking with an employee who spoke broken English. I had no baggage claim numbers so I was asked to describe my bags—black and grey. This couldn't be good! I finished filing the report in hopes that something would turn up! Somewhere! Somehow!

Afterward, I exited customs hoping to see Andy...hoping that he had waited all that time. I saw Jordan (Jo) first (Andy's Chinese friend that I met the previous summer in DC). Andy had gone downstairs but soon came walking toward us in the empty airport. We hugged, and I filled them in on my sad luggage story.

We hung out with Jo briefly in a lounge at the airport. I don't remember much of the conversation but I remember Andy giving me a Chinese name-HongHua, *Red Flower*. I liked it. Jo didn't think it was all that great. I practiced some of my Chinese with them, and Jo thought I was decent. Yay! With Jo's help, Andy and I boarded a bus at 9PM to head to Qinhuangdao. There were only a few of us on the bus. Andy and I talked a lot and I gave him his Ohio State University calendar as a Christmas gift...feeling badly that some of his other gifts did not arrive with me.

We arrived around 12:30AM to the Vaughn's apartment where I would be staying. The inside door wouldn't open so Andy called and woke them up. They were great and very friendly. They showed me the boys' room, where I would be sleeping. I feel terribly that I came bearing no gifts, thanks to the luggage situation. Andy said, "Maybe you're here this week to 'receive' blessings instead of 'give' them." I thought that was very wise. Andy gave me a little homemade stocking (so cute) with a magnet, KitKats, a red wallet full of yuan (Chinese money) and his address and a picture of Elsie (my niece) and me. What a blessing! I still feel so unsure with stuff in regards to Andy and I, our friendship, our affection. I'm just not sure what God's doing. I care so much about Andy and am blessed in so many ways by our friendship but I'm confused as to whether we're to be more than that. Is it fear? Am I scared to be with someone else? Is it a control issue? Am I not called to marriage? Am I not called to Andy? How does all that stuff happen? I want Andy to lead us in this but yet I also find myself wanting the control. Maybe it also has to do with Andy telling me about his friends, Drew and Megan, getting engaged already. They're moving so fast! I couldn't believe it. They've only just started dating it seems!? This also weirds me out a little. Should I tell Andy all this stuff? I'm thinking yes, but when and how? I want to love him as more than a friend but I think it will take much more time. I want him to know ALL about me and my family and life and *everything* before we would decide on stuff like that.

Lord, I need you to guide me this week. Tell me what to do in regards to the whole situation. You haven't closed this door with Andy so lead us, and me, through it. I don't know what I'm doing. I need you to calm my spirit and work in me this week. May I be a 'receiver' and not a 'giver' and may I be grateful in that! Amen.

DECEMBER 31, 2008

I come to meet Heather and the Vaughns around 10AM. We hang out until lunch. We eat lunch with them and then off to class… I've never been more nervous teaching a class than I was that day. I thought my students would be excited to have a visitor but they seemed shy and perhaps apathetic. How could they be apathetic? Heather Grice is in their classroom…wake up people! Four hours later I was glad that class was over. Heather and I then headed for the Korean place for dinner to meet up with Alex and Annalese (American teacher friends). We sat in a private room reserved for the four of us…pretty cozy. After dinner, we headed for the apartment of Mark and Carrie Roddy. I love the Roddys. They've become good friends of mine and Heather would stay in their spare room this night. It would be a late night as another teacher friend, Candice, invited us to celebrate New Year's Eve at her apartment. This is where Heather would meet many of the ELT Teachers. It could have been awkward for Heather not knowing people but she did great! During our prayer time, around eleven, Dayu (a Chinese sister) came and treated us by joining in the prayer time in her native tongue. I like hearing someone pray in another language. Heather and I outlasted most of the younger crowd and left the apartment around 1AM. I stayed in the ELT Edge apartment this night with other male teachers. I went to sleep grateful for the blessings in 2008.

The last day of the year! Hard to believe I woke up around 5AM…couldn't get back to sleep. I'll chalk it up to jet-lag. I overheard Brad and Carrie's family devotional time before the kids went to school. So cute! I got out of bed at 7:30AM. I ate a clementine and toast for breakfast, with some tea too, while visiting with the Chinese babysitter and Carrie. So far, so good. Everyone has been amazing. I don't know what the day holds exactly but I think the plan is lunch here, Andy's classes from 2-6pm, then to the other school for a New Year's Eve bash with Americans. I'm looking forward to it.

JANUARY 1, 2009

The early hours of 2009 beckon us to the first sunrise of the year…The beautiful sunrise would be a sign of things to come. At first, I didn't think the sun would shine through the fog/smog resting on the water before us. To our delight, around 7:20AM, the sunlight blasted through the smog. If you didn't want to look directly into the sun all you needed was to look just below the sun and see it's reflection off the ocean water. Minutes later we walked down the beach, found the Roddys and headed back to their apartment. I rested for a few minutes and then sneaked out to find seven pairs of socks and hopefully eight red flowers to give Heather for her seventh and eighth days of Christmas. I wanted to buy quality socks, but I couldn't find the sock vender. I settled for thin socks. On the way back to the apartment I saw a man carrying flowers. I became nervous. I knew I wanted to buy Heather flowers but I was afraid she may not receive them. On the other hand, I thought this was pretty random to see someone carrying flowers at just the right time that I needed to buy them. I made it all the way back to the apartment. I looked in the apartment and no one seemed to be awake. I went back out to look for the flower shop. My Chinese is limited, but I knew how to say red flower. That's Heather's name so I knew how to say it. Luckily for me, the flower shop was not far away. I picked out eight of them and put them in my bag for the evening. Originally, I thought I would give them to her at club that night. I thought the students would get a kick out of it. Plans changed as the club room wouldn't be available this night. Looking back, I'm glad I was able to give them to Heather over dinner. As for the socks, I didn't want to give Heather the socks in front of the others, so I peeked in her room and handed them to her. How fun it was to see her 'over the top excitement' over that small gift. ☺

Next, off to ice chair skating (popular in China). Weeks earlier I wrote to Heather about some mittens that I wanted her to have. Today her hands were cold. She said that she didn't need the mittens but eventually she gave in and wore one of the mittens. She laughed a lot that afternoon. Amy, Mark, Carrie, Heather and I played, raced, and took lots of pictures.

Blue Divider -that's the name we gave to the restaurant where we would go for lunch. It's called the Blue Divider because the restaurant used big blue dividers to separate the tables. All the tables were being used that day so we got to eat in the open, non-heated, garage in the dead of winter…awesome!

After visiting with some students, it was time for dinner…just Heather and me. The restaurant we went to was located down a dirt alley, but the inside was cozy. At dinner I explained to Heather that the previous seven days of gifts represented the first seven days of the 12 days of Christmas and now it was time for day eight. I said something to the effect of, "When you first came to China, I gave you the name Hong Hua, which means red flower. The Olympics in China kicked off on 8-8-08. Eight is a lucky number in China and I feel lucky to be with you. So here are eight Red Flowers." On our way back to the Vaughn's we stopped at Forest Park…a.k.a. an old people's playground. Heather and I have been to lots of parks, even our first two dates we visited Wheeling Park and then Oglebay Park. I wanted to ask Heather into a relationship on this night but I was pretty nervous and didn't want to ruin what seemed to be like a perfect day.

(I have two pages written in regards to this date but a lot of it is already recorded in Andy's…so I'll just fill in some blanks from my journal)

Great day! Wow! It started at the party at Candace's apartment last night. It was fun and I met the rest of the American teachers. We had dinner beforehand with Alex and his girlfriend Annalese from Calvin College. We went to a Korean restaurant and I did okay with the chopsticks! ☺ Yay!

I stayed the night at Mark and Carrie Roddy's apartment. They are wonderful! We planned to watch the sunrise at 7:27AM. We woke up at 6AM, checked the Pitt football score on-line, and taxied to the beach. The sunrise was beautiful. There were about sixty people already there…it was very cold! We saw one guy swimming in his speedo! Brrr!

Ice chairing [see pic at end of book] and the Blue Divider restaurant for lunch were lots of fun! Later we met up with some of Andy's students from last year where I talked with a student named Hannah. What a blessing.

Afterward Andy and I walked a bit alone and he took me to this really great coffee shop called BeiBei's for dinner. He shared with me about my "Twelve Days of Christmas Gifts!" Wow! I had no idea this had been going on since Christmas!

Day 1: December 25- One phone message
Day 2: December 26- Two text messages (from Luke and Levi)
Day 3: December 27- Three questions in an e-mail
Day 4: December 28- Four hours of prayer
Day 5 & Day 6: December 30-stocking full of six things *(Andy was off the hook for day five because I totally skipped it in flight to China)*
Day 7: December 31- Seven pairs of socks
Day 8: January 1, 2009- Eight red flowers

He gave me both seven and eight today. I had said how I didn't have socks in my carry-on luggage so it was cool that he loaded me up with seven pairs. He gave me the name 'Red Flower' in Chinese so that was the reason for the red flowers. He told me how he loved seeing my *joy* in the day and how *his cup runneth over*! He was so nervous about it all, that I was just blown away. We then walked toward one of his favorite parks in China, Forest Park. He had me shut my eyes and hold his arm as he led me to a cool spot. I trusted him but was also nervous because I wasn't sure what he was expecting from me. Upon opening my eyes, I was really excited because the park was beautiful, even in the winter...lots of lights, lots of landscaping and sculptures and fun things representing the Olympics. It was amazing. The coolest part of the park was the 'adult playground' section. It was sweet and we played on most all of the equipment. (We need these in America!) He walked me back to the Vaughn's. I was still very confused and wondering what God's plan was for this whole situation? Is there equal chemistry between us? After such a great, romantic day, you'd think I'd melt in his arms. I think I need to talk to someone but whom? Another great part of the day was that I got my baggage claim numbers from my mom in an e-mail. She mentioned Delta said the bags were in China. Whether or not I get them is a different story though. We'll see. I'm so tired.

JANUARY 2, 2009

I woke up today sooo tired. I am exhausted. It's the end of the semester and for whatever reason I can't seem to function this morning. I decided to call Brad and let him know I would arrive late to his apartment this morning and to pass this on to Heather. I eventually dragged myself out of bed and walked down the busy street to the Vaughn's. Heather was bright eyed waiting for me with a smile…looking great! This wasn't very nice of me to be so late. Yet, she was gracious and forgave my tardiness. Actually, I was a whole hour late!

The big event of this day was our travel to the Great Wall of China. I wanted to tell Heather my thoughts about us the day before and certainly I didn't want to put this off another day. This isn't an easy thing for me to talk about. I'm nervous and lacking confidence. We made our way to the Great Wall. I wanted to ask Heather if she would hold my hand as we stepped onto the wall. I didn't. My confidence was weak. Heather didn't seem too impressed by the Wall. Furthermore, I didn't think she was too impressed with me either. Conversation seemed uneasy for me. Yet, I really wanted to tell her my thoughts from the past few months and how I believed God was preparing us for one another. We didn't make it even a fourth of the way up the wall and I believed Heather had seen enough. We decided to turn around and head back. Finally, as we walked off the Great Wall, I timidly fumbled out some of my thoughts about us. I don't think I expressed myself very well. Yet Heather seemed to understand. I wanted us to make some kind of commitment to one another. She wasn't in agreement. It wasn't the right time for her. We continued to talk for another hour or so. I have never tasted something so bitter sweet. I was having a real 'heart to heart' conversation with Heather…so sweet. Yet I was being shut out from getting too close to her heart which seemed to be as guarded as the Great Wall of China we had visited that day…bitter!

Am I foolish? All this time I thought Heather was coming here to see me. Maybe she just wanted to see China? Perhaps she came to China to know me better and I haven't performed well enough.

With all that was said today, I still believe that Gad has special plans for Heather and me. I understand she needs time. I respect her decision, but I'm a bit baffled by how things have gone so far. I will pray and trust in His will. I seem to have two choices in front of me… be sad or cling to His promise in Romans 8:28, "And we know that in all things God works for the good of those who love him, who have been called according to his purpose."

JANUARY 3, 2009

Yesterday was great but a little rough. I woke up at 3AM and couldn't fall back asleep. I just kept replaying in my head what I needed to say to Andy. I knew I wanted to tell him my fears of intimacy and how I was still confused about us and that my heart hasn't caught up with my mind. Andy finally arrived at 9:30AM. He was supposed to be there at 8:30AM. I was a little worried but it worked out. After hanging out for a little bit I brought up how I couldn't believe we hadn't heard anything about my luggage. Then he mentioned Air China had called him that morning and told him they had my luggage. I was surprised. Why didn't Andy share this with me right away? Didn't he know how concerned I was about the lost luggage? I was confused and unimpressed…but I didn't let it ruin another great day in China.

After leaving the Vaughn's and sharing a meal with some of Andy's students, we were on our way to see the Great Wall.

We rode two buses and caught a ride in a small three-wheeled car to take us to the Wall. We felt badly because we couldn't communicate with the driver. The Wall was really neat though and we had fun. On the walk back down, Andy shared about what he wanted/saw for his future…family, kids, ministry, etc. I was quiet, and then I felt it was the time the Lord wanted me to share my feelings. I basically vomited everything up that I wanted to say and had been rehearsing in my mind. We had to awkwardly pause the conversation for the taxi ride back down to the city (since I sat in front, and Andy was in the back). After we paid, we started to walk toward a bus stop (it was maybe a 10-minute lapse of silence) …then we talked about LOTS of stuff. I was very honest as usual. He shared about his past dates and relationships since I mentioned mine (or lack thereof). I was starting to feel more comfortable. We kept walking, passing several bus stops, and kept up with our open conversation. I grabbed his arm and we walked as he shared. I enjoy hearing his stories. He stopped me at one point and said 'You'll have to take a leap of faith at some point.' I thought this was well said. I definitely have some control issues. At one point he also asked if I wanted gift #9 (of the 12 Days of Christmas Gifts). I told him that after what I shared, I didn't expect him to give me any more gifts. He told me the ninth day was nine words and that he wanted to share them… *"You're wonderfully and fearfully made and just be patient."* Count them. He's right…nine! The first part of this is from Psalm 139 so I know they are words from God and not just Andy. These nine words really spoke to me (and continued to resonate in me the remainder of the trip).

After transferring to a second bus to Qinhuangdao, it was getting really cold so we sat close together… our sides next to each other. It was fun because at one point we switched so our opposing sides could get warmed! I liked it. So, is he to be more than a friend? We returned and had dinner with the Vaughns after they put the kids to bed. We talked with them until 10:45PM. We found out the Hokies won the Orange Bowl 20–7. Andy left, and I went to bed happy to have a clearer mind.

JANUARY 4, 2009

Today we woke up early and headed to the school to make breakfast for Andy's team…French toast and eggs. We talked with Carrie about my lost luggage and finally decided it would be best to have Air China mail my luggage to their apartment. I left Carrie a list of stuff that was in the luggage and what belonged to whom for when they did the sorting.

JANUARY 6, 2009

(For some reason I don't journal again until Jan 6th but I do try to recap the trip to Langfang/Beijing on this day.)

We were headed to Langfang via the fast train and a taxi ride from Beijing. The train station was the first place that I felt out-of-place as a foreigner in China. Andy and I were the only non-Chinese people there. I felt many eyes on us. On the train Andy shared multiple times how he was just so excited to be with me and beside me. He also shared with me how from our conversation with Brad and Carrie he realized that I am superior to him intellectually. He followed that up by saying he hopes he makes up for it through his basketball skills! Haha! ☺ I laughed. How cute is he? This cracked me up! He's awesome! I assured him that he was gifted in many other ways. He seemed confident as he shared even though I felt as if I might have broken his heart the previous day. Was the Lord telling him something different?

After an expensive cab ride, we made it safely to see our mutual YL friend, Jess Shamblee, and her team in Langfang,

China. In the cab, Andy gave me gift ten—ten pieces of chocolate. Yum! Sunday morning, we had breakfast with Jess then met up with the team for worship. Jess Distad (a teammate of Jess Shamblee), shared from Isaiah 6 and the death of something in order to see a secondary vision. It made me think that maybe I needed to die to the relationship with Andy? I kept wondering what Andy was hearing the whole time. Later, when we were alone, he said he didn't have many thoughts on that part of it. Andy seemed kind of distant that afternoon before we all met to go to the Agape orphanage. I didn't know what to do or say. The orphanage was a blast and it was all thanks to Andy who had found it. I was so proud of him. I was able to share a little bit with Shamblee that evening in how confused I felt while she listened.

Monday morning Andy and I went for a walk and we didn't say too much more. He gave me some scriptures to read, eleven of them for gift eleven, and followed it up by saying he wouldn't be giving me gift twelve just yet...maybe next year? We talked about less contact with each other in January, or maybe for a few weeks, ten days, or so. Who knows?

That afternoon we took a train ride with Shamblee into Beijing for the night. We registered at the hostel then did some site-seeing (Tiananmen Square, Forbidden City, Silk Market, and Texas Pete's for dinner). At the Silk Market I set my VT ski cap down somewhere. I didn't realize it until we were at the subway but as soon as I told Andy he said he'd go back and look for it...so sweet. I bought some souvenirs for my family and Andy helped by bargaining for some ornaments. Originally the lady wanted 220 yuan. Andy helped me get them for 80 yuan. I was definitely impressed and very proud of his bargaining skills. That night we talked a little bit more before I went to bed...my last night in China. We didn't discuss anything new, just lots of thanksgiving on both our parts for a great week.

On Tuesday, Jess, Andy, and I checked out of the hostel and

headed for a quick visit with Chinese friends, Tony and Lily, on the way to the airport. They are adorable and Ximei (their baby daughter) is precious. When we asked Tony to share his testimony, he mostly shared about meeting Lily and after seven days proposing to her and their story. They took a leap of faith. I was thinking, as he shared, if this was God telling me to take my own leap of faith with Andy? I had remembered Andy telling me about taking a leap of faith a few days ago.

The three of us rode the subway to the airport and hung out until 11:45am before hugging goodbye. It went well and I was fine. I'm sure it must have been tougher on Andy though, but he seemed okay. I know he cares for me so much.

Chapter 15

BACK TO MY FIRST LOVE

I humbled myself with fasting

—PSALM 35:13

The next few pages are excerpts from my journal entries from the ten days after my return from China. I had decided I would 'fast' Andy (and he fasted as well). I would not e-mail, write, text, or call him for ten days. Instead, I would spend the time praying and drawing closer to my first love, Jesus.

I came home from China very confused (and without my luggage).

As I shared with Andy before I left, I felt like my mind was saying 'yes, Andy,' while my heart was saying either 'no,' or 'not yet.' Now he had asked three times about our friendship being more. Each time I couldn't say yes. He was great, of course, and listened, and seemed to take it all in and understand. After much conversation on both our parts there was a moment where he stopped me and said "at some point, you're just going to have to take a leap of faith." I was blown away by this and told him I knew this was from God. Ultimately, I knew in relationships there comes a point when you just have to have faith—whether it's with Andy or whoever. I thanked him for the words. I'm not sure if he was brokenhearted by the things I said, but he definitely didn't show it if he was. Before I left for home, he mentioned that he thinks maybe God is giving me cautious feelings since he still wouldn't be back from China until July? Valid point. I had also mentioned to Andy how I thought I needed to go on an 'Andy fast' for a couple weeks or forty days once I was home. I decided I would not e-mail or write him during the 'Andy fast.' When I would think of him, I was going to do my best to turn those thoughts into thoughts of God instead. (I hoped anyway.) Andy suggested a ten day fast and I agreed. I talked to my good, Christian girlfriend, Roseann, and she gave me advice. She shared when she has a decision to make in her life and she doesn't sense God telling her one way or the other, she does nothing and waits. She thought the 'fast' idea was a good one.

Of course, this was all even more confusing because I've never had a guy in my life before and I didn't (and still don't know) what to feel or do.

JANUARY 8, 2009

My friend, Boo, encouraged me in the fast (via e-mail) and said to journal about all of it. She said she'd be praying that God would speak clearly to me and that He would give me a word or scripture to cling to each day. I was confused when today's scripture was Psalm 34:18, "The Lord is near to those with a broken heart…" It made me think that I was going to break Andy's heart with too harsh of a decision. The Lord also gave me Psalm 36… *"Your faithfulness reaches to the skies…"* **I knew that God would be faithful to me in the fast.**

JANUARY 9, 2009

"Delight yourself in the Lord and He will give you the desires of your heart." –Psalm 37:4

I had talked with many people by the time January 9th had come around and my heart was starting to make a turn. Some friends who had given me advice mentioned trust and communication as keys to a relationship. Andy and I have that. I had also looked through my China pictures and saw that in all of the ones of Andy, he looked like such a cutie. (Why did he say he wasn't photogenic?) One of the biggest things of this day, however, was when I did a search for Andy's profile on Facebook. It did not show up. He must have inactivated it. Wow! I'm not sure of his exact reason(s) for taking it down, but to me, I felt like he was really taking the 'fast' serious for me and wanted to fast himself possibly. (Obviously I was doing poorly at the "Andyfast" that day by searching for his profile.) This simple act convicted me of the man that God created Andy to be. He is prayerful and intentional. By the end of the day, I was encouraged to see what more God would share with me in regards to a relationship with Andy throughout the fast. It was also a day where I really contemplated just sending him an e-mail 'Hello.' But I abstained.

JANUARY 10, 2009

Psalm 40 "I waited patiently for the Lord; He turned to me and heard my cry."

In my journal this day I write, **"...draw me close to him (Andy) in every way...help me to care for him as a wife does her husband... if it's Your will of course...or shut this door completely, Lord... Guide me and draw me closer to You through it all."**

JANUARY 11, 2009

Andy sent out a mass e-mail today saying that he's doing well and his cup overflows. (It was written to about 15 people or so and included me). He was obviously confident in God's plan, while I was still wondering. I journaled, **"I need to put my focus back on loving Christ, though! Not worrying about the other stuff!" The Lord gave me Psalm 20 "May He answer you when you are in distress, may He give you the desire of your heart" and Psalm 42 "As the deer pants for the water…" help me to pant for you, Lord.**

JANUARY 12, 2009

Psalm 46 "Be still and know that I am God."

JANUARY 14, 2009

It was getting harder and harder for me not to think about Andy. Keri (my college roommate for four years) had e-mailed me, "you think too much and are the most logical person I know." She added, "love is not logical." These words hit me hard because Keri knows me very well. Andy's mom also called today and asked me how the trip went. She had not talked to Andy yet. I began to wonder when Andy would call me since he mentioned something about 'a ten day fast.' This would end Jan 16th. I was praying for God to give me words to speak when Andy called. I jotted a few things down that I definitely wanted to tell him—"thanks for: your patience, that you care for me in my psycho-ness, twelve days of Christmas, your kind words, the money you spent and all the plans you made, remembering my luggage (he had e-mailed a thank you to Mom and Meghan for Christmas gifts where he mentioned the luggage would arrive by the Superbowl), flowers, words, scripture, bargaining at the market, your smile."

JANUARY 15, 2009

"I know there's more for us [Andy and me] ...but I'm not sure what these next six months will look like however, or how we'll talk about them? It's cool not knowing when he'll call me but also distracting. Probably not the best thing when I'm trying to fast from thoughts of him and towards thoughts of my Savior and first love! Don't let me give you verbiage, Lord! Draw me to You!"

Psalm 50:7 "Hear... and I will speak!"
Psalm 51:12 "Grant me a willing spirit to sustain me."
Psalm 52:9 "In Your Name I will hope..."

Chapter 16

AN ANSWER

If you remain in me and my words remain in you,
ask whatever you wish and it will be given you.

—JOHN 15:7

January 16, 2009, Friday-The Coolest Day of
2009-literally (-15°) and figuratively

Throughout the fast I'd been praying and finally came to the realization that I care about Andy so much. I want to spend more time with him to see what God has planned. I remembered today would be the tenth day of our fast, so I was expecting a phone call from Andy.

Mom called me at school while I was at lunch and said a package arrived at their house for me. She wanted me to grab it on my way home. I asked her if it was from China, (possibly my luggage?). She said she didn't know because it didn't say. Then I just figured it might be from my friends in Spain or something, so whatever. I went about the rest of my day.

I got to my parents' house around 4:15PM and walked in the basement door. I saw my luggage and another black bag inside the door. My luggage had arrived! So fun. I started walking it up the basement steps and yelled to Mom in the kitchen, "I guess you just had to open the box before I got here to see that it was my luggage, huh?" She smiled and said "yeah." I talked briefly with her and Jed (my brother who was there too) ...while my dad was napping on the living room floor. I opened the luggage to check things out, but Mom stopped me and told me the *actual* package I got was in her car. The luggage was the *other* package for me, so I should go get the one in the car. I was confused. I walked down the basement steps and got closer to the glass doors (where the blinds were shut) ...

and then I saw the back of Andy standing outside of it. I COULDN'T BELIEVE IT!! UNBELIEVABLE! WOW! I immediately went out (so overwhelmed with the whole situation) and gave him a big hug and was excited. I couldn't believe he was HERE...in the US of A!!? At MY parents' house...not his parents'!? He was just in China for Pete's sake!! I had him give me the basic info: He arrived late Thursday night and stayed at a friend's house (Chris Buda). He told *no one*, except Chris, about the entire trip!! Not even his mom or dad or brothers!! It was a complete shock and surprise to *all* of us. I was blown away. It was like straight from a fairy tale!! How did I get such an amazing guy to care about me so much? I know—only by the grace of God! :)

I felt good and was happy to realize that I was excited to see him. My soul was joyful he was here and glad he had kept it from me as a surprise. Now, before you go and judge him and think it was all Andy's doing... guess when he booked the flight to come home? He did not book it after I left him in China as you may be thinking.

He booked it in *October*!! He had this trip planned *way* before I even bought my flight to China!! Andy was even contemplating what to do about telling me he was coming or not. But he decided against it because he wanted to surprise all of us!! Wow!! Completely *unbelievable*!!

This is God and His amazing provision, and providence. I couldn't have asked for a better day or month!! Andy is now here until Feb 12th and I couldn't be happier. I'm *truly* looking forward to all the good times we will have while he's here.

FEBRUARY 10, 2009

The four weeks with Andy have come and gone and now it's time for us to say 'see you later' once more. The past twenty-six days have been a lot of fun and we've learned much more about one another. On Jan 19th (MLK Jr. Day -No School for WGHS) we took a cold walk from Mom and Dad's house with Rocko (the family collie dog). At one point I remember sharing with Andy that I didn't want another girl to get *my* Andy Nelson, and that I thought about him all the time. He stopped me, looked in my eyes and asked something like, "so are you saying you'd like to be my intimate friend?" I think I said 'yeah' or something to that effect. We hugged. He asked if he could kiss me on the forehead. We walked a little further and talked and clarified that 'intimate friend' meant we would be exclusively dating. I felt confident in God's plan so I was on board.

We hugged again and finished our walk back to my parents'—excited about what it meant, but also shocked of where God had taken us in a matter of weeks. I remember especially being blessed by Andy flowering me with compliments that he'd held back sharing until our friendship grew. These were things I've never heard before like 'you're amazing, you're attractive, and you're a miracle.' He also shared how the best thing about me was my 'love for the Lord first and foremost.' Wow! Since that walk Andy has continued to bless me with kind words, fun stories, poems, texts, e-mails, notes, a song he wrote for me, and quality time.

Some other highlights from those four weeks include going to the Oglebay YL leader weekend *together*, watching the Steelers win the Super Bowl, hanging out more with friends and family, and playing board games.

I can't forget to mention the twelfth gift (from the twelve days of Christmas gifts he gave me in China). A few days after our walk on Jan 19th, I received a card in the mail from Andy. It was a sweet, romantic note of joy and thankfulness. It included some yellow post-it notes as well. Later Andy pointed out to me that I should count the notes. Twelve. Also, the card was signed *"Love, Andy."* This was the first time Andy's salutation would say, "Love, Andy". This final gift of the "twelve days" appropriately came via snail mail and was handwritten by my favorite guy. I wouldn't have wanted it any other way.

I'm in awe of how God is working in my heart. I know there is a lot more in store for Andy and me and I'm excited to see where He takes us on this journey toward abundant life.

Chapter 17

PHONE CALLS

Call to me and I will answer you and tell you
great and unsearchable things you do not know.

—JEREMIAH 33:3

A ndy's return flight for China was set for February 12, 2009.
He would be finishing his second and final year of teaching in
Qinhuangdao. He would be back in the states soon enough, but it
seemed like a long way off. Andy spent the night prior at my parents'
house and I requested the morning off from work so I could drive
him to the airport. We waited by the security check point for half
an hour and talked small talk. We didn't want to focus on being
apart for the next four months. I was again getting nervous about
being affectionate as we said goodbye. I wasn't sure what Andy
would expect and if I would be comfortable with public displays of
affection. In the end, we walked up to security and we hugged. He
kissed me on the forehead. I could see he was doing his best to hold
back tears. I was okay and tried to be tough for the both of us. He
walked through the lines and beyond the metal detectors. I watched
as he walked away and we waved again one last time. It was best to
think of it as a *see you later* rather than a *goodbye*. We had much to
look forward to as he boarded one last time for China.

Throughout those next four months we had weekly skype calls.
We also continued writing letters and e-mails. I did not have a webcam
so most all our conversations were voice only. I looked forward to
hearing from Andy often, and I know he appreciated it too. I also stayed

connected with Andy's family and would call his grandmother and Dad occasionally to say hello and let them know I was thinking about them.

Time flew by and before I knew it, May had arrived and I was going to be turning thirty years old. In early May I received the perfect card from Andy. It was from the Christian bookstore in China and had real, dried, red flowers on it, with the verse, *Be joyful always,* in Chinese and English. Wow! What a perfect card for me as I love that verse. Inside the card Andy wished me happy birthday and told a short story of what he chose for his Chinese name. (He had given me the name Honghua or Red Flower as you may remember).

Be joyful always
(1Th 5:16)

要常常喜樂 (帖前 5:16)

Hi Heather ☺

*Happy Birthday from China!! I miss you!! I like you!!
Do you want to know the meaning of my Chinese
name? I will tell you, but first I will comment about
the front of this card. The red flower is beautiful and
that is why I chose it for your name. The red flower is
considered most beautiful and so it seemed appropriate
that you would have this name. As I look at the front
of this card, I think of how lucky is the green leaf. The
green leaf gets to collect water to give to the red flower.
Best of all the green leaf spends his life near the red
flower. How lucky? What friendship! What romance?
What a blessing for the green leaf. Thanks for listening
to my story and if you haven't guessed, my Chinese
name is… Lu Ye, or Green Leaf.*

*Love, Andy
P.S. Happy Four Months!!*

I melted. How *romantic*. How *sweet*. What an amazing card
from an amazing guy!

I didn't expect anything else, but on the actual day of my 30th
birthday I received a phone call in the morning from him before
heading off to work. During the school day, I heard from the
office that I had received flowers, but when I picked them up, I
was surprised they were from Meghan and Jace (not Andy). It was
still great! However, when I came home from school, I had a box
of a dozen colorful roses and some chocolates awaiting me at the
door—from Andy. Wow! Finally, that evening, he called some of
his students over to his building to sing *happy birthday* to me on
skype (in Chinese and English)! It was my favorite birthday by far!
I felt really loved and special. I still have a big smile thinking about
it years later!

Chapter 18

RETURN FROM CHINA, PART II

He is altogether lovely. This is my
beloved, and this is my friend.

—SONG OF SONGS 5:16

Andy was scheduled to come home on June 29th, and I was so looking forward to meeting him upon arrival. Early in June I began to imagine what it would be like to reunite at the airport. I had it planned out that I would show up with a balloon for him that had an elephant drawn on it. It would be just like one of his students had made him earlier in the year (her apology gift to him since she broke down crying and couldn't give her speech in class). I thought it would be a great laugh, but also let him know how special he is to me. I was also nervous how that scene would actually play out and what expectations he might have for meeting me at the airport. (Can you see how I think too much?)

Prior to his arrival, I was finishing up an educational field trip with students in Spain until June 24th. My grandma picked me up at the airport and took me home. I needed to rest before leaving for a YL teacher weekend in Rockbridge, Virginia, a few days later.

As we pulled into the farm lane, we saw a kid walking. It looked like he had something in his hand. I made a comment to Grandma that it looked like someone was walking up to come visit her. As we got closer, I thought it looked like Andy. It **was** Andy! So wild! He was walking up the lane toward my house to surprise me there. He wasn't sure what time I'd be home, but he had only arrived from

China the night previous. He was jet-lagged just as much as I was. He also had a cast on his hand.

> The short version of that goes something like this: The week prior he was playing basketball with some students in China. He went to take the ball from a kid and somehow broke a bone in his hand in the process. The Chinese wanted to operate and put a plate in. Andy thought he'd better get a second opinion so he talked to some family and my mom (who is a nurse). From looking at some e-mailed x-rays it was decided that Andy could probably just get a cast and be fine. It was best to receive the cast in America since he'd be going home soon. Would he be able to bump his flight up since he needed medical help? He did. The next few days for him were full of goodbyes and cleaning up to leave a country after two years of teaching. Things came together quickly, and he made it home to the U.S. by the grace of God and many people helping him along the way. It's important to note that the airlines lost his luggage (go figure). At least he didn't have that to juggle with only one, good hand. He flew home and arrived back in Pittsburgh on June 23rd. Our friend, Chris, picked him up at the airport and the next day Mom met him to take him to an urgent care place for x-rays. He was scheduled for a doctor's appointment the following day.

I was again surprised to see him back in the USA but it wasn't as unbelievable as last time. *He's always full of surprises it seems.* He got in the back of the car and Grandma drove us the rest of the way to my house. He helped unload my luggage (with one hand of course),

Grandma left, and then we hugged and began to catch up from the past two weeks (my trip to Spain, his final days in China).

The next day was pretty funny! I accompanied him to his doctor's appointment and had to fill out all kinds of paperwork for him (since he couldn't write). He fractured his left hand and happens to be left-handed. I learned a lot about his health and medical history and, from what I heard, so did my mom who helped him the day prior. He was given a cast and then we were off to the Cootes' house in West Greene for Young Life Campaigners (a weekly Bible study for teens which Jon and Maribeth Coote graciously hosted). I was looking forward to seeing the kids and to talk about Spain but also for them to meet Andy. I loved it—finally my two worlds were coming together! I was most impressed with Andy's intentionality with the kids. He had been praying their names with me for two years, and finally he was meeting a few of them face to face. As soon as the kids said their names, Andy would follow it with guessing their last names. I was amazed. What a great guy!

That weekend was tough because I had to leave Andy... again. I took three teacher friends with me to a Young Life teacher conference in Virginia. I was able to call him a few times, but I was definitely looking forward to coming home and spending more time together.

Andy was at my house when I returned from the conference on June 28th. Later that night we sat outside on my porch and talked more about us and what he was thinking about for his future job. He told me nervously that he had thoughts of us being in China down the road. He didn't know a time-frame, but he wanted me to know. I assured him that my future was with him, and how I wanted him to go where God was leading. I would follow. It was one of those things I just said and then later thought more about. *Was I really ready to follow him and leave this life I've lived for the past few years?* It would be something I'd be prayerful about for the next few months. I was gaining confidence in God's plan, however.

It was around that same time that Andy gave me a pretty intimate letter to read stating something like *"I'm not sure you could ever*

possibly care for me as deeply as I care for you…and this concerns me…
but God is a God of the impossible and I'll trust Him." I understood
why Andy was writing this. It was true, but it also broke my heart.
I began to pray more and more—asking God to work on my heart
in a mighty way. I asked Him to please help me to fall for this
amazing guy with my whole heart… to want him as a wife wants a
husband…to care for him as much as he cared for me. I took some
time to write Andy a letter in return. I gave him an analogy to help
him understand where I felt I was coming from.

> Over the years I've built this so-called *brick wall*
> with regards to relationships with guys. The wall is
> pretty sturdy, built on a solid foundation of Christ
> to protect my heart. The wall has only ever had
> windows in it, with me looking out at guys and
> admiring them from afar. Then a few years ago,
> Andy asked me out and I decided I'd put in a door
> (so to speak). That was good enough for me. We
> would date and spend time together, but nothing
> else too deep where my heart could be affected.
> Then he came back from China and I realized that
> a relationship takes more than doors and windows
> in a brick wall. The only way to move forward was
> for the brick wall to come down. But this brick wall
> could not be taken down quickly with a wrecking
> ball or bulldozer. The bricks were too precious for
> that and still useful. It would require time, patience,
> grace, care, and love. The bricks would have to be
> taken down one at a time. I then asked Andy if he
> was willing to be like a 'bricklayer?' (I also thought
> later how the real relationship process takes bricks
> from each other's lives and creates a new masterpiece
> with bricks from both, and a foundation in Christ…
> this could be called a marriage.)

God did answer my prayers. Over the next couple of months, I completely fell in love with Bruce Andrew Nelson, a Southpaw from St. Clairsville, Ohio. It really didn't take long at all for God to work on my heart once I began to pray, have faith in Him, and trust Andy's leadership.

After Andy came back from China, there were many times when my heart started to melt and bricks started to come down. In early July Andy helped me volunteer at a Vacation Bible School near West Greene High School. He even played games with the kids. I liked watching him run around and laugh with the others. On July 4th, Andy humbly surprised us all by coming in second place in the family competition of ten people running the Whiskey Rebellion 5K! I was also encouraged to have Andy cheer me on as I came in tenth. Ha! Later, Andy said one thing he liked most about the day was seeing me run to the finish still smiling and joyful (even if I was sweaty and red-faced).

During our big Grice reunion picnic that day, Andy met lots of the family and talked and visited with most all of them. He didn't need me to be by his side at all times, which I appreciated. I was so encouraged by him this day. It also helped that the family was falling in love with him too and told me so. I remember I kissed him on the cheek in saying goodbye that night.

On July 7th Mom invited everyone over so we could celebrate Andy's birthday (a little late) in America! We had a yummy American meal, played cards, and then hung out later after mom and dad went to bed. We watched some old YL videos and some other old videos Mom had of me. I enjoyed sitting beside him on the couch and smiled happily while we whispered to not wake anyone up.

July 11th was a *huge* day for my heart! We were set to see the play, *Les Miserables,* at 2PM in Pittsburgh. Andy picked me up around noon and looked so handsome. (He smelled amazing too.) We got Wendy's drive thru for lunch and we took it to a rest area picnic table to eat outside. I sat to his right and while eating I remember him commenting that he was glad to be sitting on the left side of me since the wind was blowing that way (this way he could smell me). I was flattered.

The play was good, but just holding hands with Andy and being together was better. The rest of the day was a dream as we walked in the city, sat on park benches, put our feet in the water, laughed, fed the squirrels, drove to Primanti Brothers' restaurant, returned to Mom and Dad's house, sat on the porch swing, walked in the field, and danced under the moonlight. (I'm excited just typing it out as a memory.)

On July 15th Andy drove me around Jamboree in the Hills, and then we went for a long walk in Barkamp Park. I doubt Andy remembers it, but at one point during this walk I asked him where he saw himself in two years. He answered "with you" and then asked me in a serious, whispering voice, "Are we talking seriously now?" I smiled and we didn't say much else about it, but inwardly I melted more. I would later admit to him how excited I was when we whispered to each other. After our walk in Barkamp and chillin' on a park bench, we went to the covered bridge pond to chat more. I liked being close to him and thumb-wrestling. It was also this day that Andy told me how after half an hour with me his brain turns to mush. Ha!

Our six-month dating anniversary was July 19th. We went to church together and then walked around Memorial Park for a bit before I went home. Mom and I then drove to Maryland to visit my sister and her family. While staying at Meghan's, Andy and I had some fun texting conversations. I remember at one point asking if I could be the third strand with him and God from Ecc. 4:12, "Though one may be overpowered, two can defend themselves. A cord of three strands is not quickly broken." Mom would later comment to Meghan how I talked about Andy a lot that weekend. I knew that I loved Andy, but I wasn't sure when and if I should tell him those words yet.

In late July, I offered to take two of my West Greene students to visit a college ministry at the University of Pittsburgh. Andy was happy to join in the fun. He drove my car and we had a good trip. After dropping off the two students we came back to my house to hang out a little more. I knew I was going to tell Andy *I love you*, this day but I wasn't sure when or how. Andy agreed to play cards with me. After a little while—I beat him in the first few rounds—we stopped, and I said something like, "I actually have something I'd like to share." I don't remember exactly, but I believe I said something to the effect of "somewhere between an e-mail in 2007 and playing cards with you tonight, I've fallen in love with you and I want you to know."

A little surprised, Andy replied, "Thanks." I don't know what I expected him to say, but I don't think I thought it would be *thanks*. He did follow it by saying something like "I feel similarly, but I'm not going to say those words right now because I think that by saying them, I should follow it up by being on bended knee." Perfect response! I was totally okay with it.

Chapter 19

ANSWERING A CALL

Go and make disciples of all nations...

—MATTHEW 28:19

In the fall of 2009 Andy was enrolled at Wheeling Jesuit University to gain his teaching certificate by the summer of 2010. While taking classes, Jerry Ebbert (a family friend/neighbor) offered Andy a job—if he wanted it—as a temporary vegetable farmer. Upon thinking about it, Andy decided it was a great opportunity to work outside and earn some extra money while finishing his teaching classes. He worked three to five days a week, and enjoyed it alot. He always had stories to share after a day's work. One of the funniest was in regard to picking tomatoes. He mentioned that the other workers were always telling him he missed picking some of the ripe tomatoes. Later he realized that his color blindness was hindering him in distinguishing the red from the green ones. Ha!

Meanwhile, in late September, a friend of ours approached us about a job opening in Waynesburg for a youth pastor at a church. This was very intriguing to us since I was working in Waynesburg at West Greene High School. Maybe the Lord was calling us to Greene County, as a couple? Andy interviewed with the church a few times, and I admit I was really wondering about it—so much so that as I drove around Waynesburg, I would catch myself looking at houses. *Could we buy one? Would we settle there doing Young Life and be involved with a youth pastor position at the same time?* It all sounded pretty magical. Andy was more guarded about the position and never really felt like it was right. We were grateful when the church decided a month later that they would not be hiring a full-time youth pastor yet. We were thankful the Lord had closed that door for us.

In similar timing, I felt the Lord telling me to prepare to leave West Greene and *go*. Many things were happening at school that allowed me to participate in *less* school-related activities (Spanish Club, class sponsor, etc.), and gave me *more* time to do Young Life and hang out with students as a friend and mentor after school. In the days and weeks that followed our trip to Virginia Tech we prayed a lot and asked God to guide us in the decision of possibly teaching in China. We spoke with friends and family and asked for more information from Newt Hetrick at IECS (International English and Cultural Studies) to work with them. I decided I should meet with Mary Beth Crouch, my close friend and fellow YL leader, to share with her about my plans for the next school year. Surprisingly, she shared first and told me she felt called to stay at West Greene for the next year. Wow, praise the Lord! When I followed up her news with "I'm likely leaving West Greene to go to China," we were both excited. I felt the Lord had lifted a worry I was having about the future of Young Life in the area. *God's plan is always good, pleasing, and perfect* (Romans 12:2).

By Thanksgiving we had told our families that we felt China was where the Lord was leading us. Mom was not very happy about it at first. In later conversations, I was able to share more in depth about IECS and how it's a ten-month teaching opportunity. We would be home for the summer. She asked me to promise her we would not live in China forever. I couldn't promise her that, but I definitely didn't feel like this would be a problem in the future. Dad was even more skeptical. He didn't understand why we would want to go to a country where sharing about Jesus is forbidden. We kept praying.

Chapter 20

TWO QUESTIONS

> For where two or three come together
> in my name, there am I with them.
>
> —MATTHEW 18:20

It was a school night and our one-year anniversary of officially being boyfriend and girlfriend (January 19, 2010). We decided this day would be the one where we would call Newt (the leader of IECS) to tell him we were officially committed to teaching in China the next school year. We decided to go to dinner at the Evergreen China Buffet in celebration of our decision. It was a casual place with good food. Andy seemed relaxed. After we came back, we decided to take a walk (just like we had in 2009). The walk was definitely warmer than it had been the year previous, and there was no snow on the ground. It was romantic, and he paused in the same spot to kiss me on the forehead as he had the year before. We stopped at my parents' house afterward since Andy had planned to stay the night there. (Mom was in Maryland with Meghan after Bridget's birth, my second niece. Dad was still at the farm milking).

We knelt in the living room to pray for our future decision to go to China. After a short time of prayer, Andy said, "Amen." I was surprised he'd ended it so soon since I know he likes to pray. He asked if I could sit on my parents' recliner while he read something to me. It was Psalm 23. He went on to explain that this Psalm had been dear to him in our dating and always spoke to him that he should not fear, for the Lord is with him.

Psalm 23

The Lord is my shepherd I shall not be in want.
He makes me lie down in green pastures, he leads
me beside quiet waters, he restores my soul.
He guides me in paths of righteousness for his name's sake.
Even though I walk through the valley of the shadow of death,
I will fear no evil for you are with me; your
rod and your staff, they comfort me.
You prepare a table for me in the presence of my enemies.
You anoint my head with oil; my cup overflows.
Surely goodness and love will follow me all the days of my
life, and I will dwell in the house of the Lord forever.

I thanked him. He then told me to shut my eyes. I could hear him looking for something. I opened my eyes, and he handed me a single, red rose. I again thanked him and said it was beautiful. He told me to keep looking at it. I didn't see anything. Then he said, "Look on the ribbon." When I finally did, I saw there was a diamond ring on it—an engagement ring. Andy was still on his knees. He took the ring and said "Heather, I love you (this was the first time he ever verbalized these words to me), I want to marry you and I want to go to China with you." I responded in typical *Heather-fashion*—humor. "So, is there a question in there?" He smiled, then asked, "Will you marry me, and will you go to China with me?" I said, "Yeah," and we had our first real kiss. ☺

We sat and talked a lot afterward and made some decisions on how we would begin telling people about our engagement. We decided to get on the internet and temporarily deactivate our Facebook accounts so no one could find out earlier than we wanted. Our first call was to Newt telling him we were set to go to China in the Fall. He was thrilled to hear of our decision to be a part of his team. Then we started making visits and calls to share our engagement news. I called Mom and Meghan (together in Maryland), then Jed and his wife, Nicole. We decided to drive to Andy's grandma's house to tell her in person. We called Andy's mom and brothers on the way while Andy drove. We visited with Andy's grandma for ten minutes before she came right out and asked "So, do you have something to tell me?" We did. She was happy for us and then we were off to Andy's parents' house to see his dad. His dad was also all smiles. It was getting to be really late by this point so Andy started to drive me back to Washington. I called Dad, too, (but of course he already knew since Andy had asked his permission and shopped for the ring with him). I was ecstatic inside, but I made a vow to not tell anyone at school until I could tell the YL campaigner kids privately after school. They were happy and felt honored to be the first from West Greene to hear the news.

After most all our close friends had received calls, we reinstated our Facebook pages with a new status—*engaged*.

Chapter 21

THE BIG DAY

Dear friends, let us love one another,
for love comes from God.

—1 JOHN 4:7

Less than six months later we had our July 4th wedding. It was everything I had ever dreamed and more. I was able to use the months between engagement and wedding to do many things in preparation.

On a snowy day (schools were canceled) in February, Mom, Nicole (my sister-in-law) and I went wedding dress shopping in Wheeling. Honestly, I was not looking forward to wedding dress shopping for the following reasons: 1) I'm cheap, 2) I have an odd shape for dresses, and 3) I didn't really feel comfortable with people doting over me to try on thousands of dresses. After picking out more than a handful of dresses to try on, I was getting discouraged that I might not find the right one. I had one more left on the hanger, and I wasn't all that excited about it. I thought maybe I shouldn't even try it. My mom encouraged me otherwise. I put it on, and it fit perfectly (minus the length of course). It was plain white, form-fitted at the waist, A-line at the bottom, and had off the shoulder sleeves. I felt like Belle from the Disney movie, *Beauty and the Beast*. Mom and Nicole liked it too. When I saw that it was on clearance ($99) I knew I would have to act that day or it could be gone. We all agreed that this was the dress and just the right thing for the soon-to-be Heather Nelson. *Sold*!

Mom and Meghan did a lot of the legwork to help us find a reception hall, and we finally settled on the McLure Hotel in Wheeling. It was the exact place of Michelle and Adam's reception from 2003 when Andy and I had first spoken. Pretty cool.

Andy and I worked hard to make many of the arrangements for the wedding ourselves. We talked a lot about where to get married and after discussing and praying about a few options, we felt Andy's home church of Thoburn United Methodist, in St. Clairsville, would be just the right place. It was the right size for the many family and friends we hoped to invite and had a great location. Most importantly, it was available on July 4th. Our good friend, Chris Buda, said he would be happy to perform the ceremony. Andy asked his brothers to be his best *men,* and I asked Meghan to be my maid of honor. To even things out, I was hopeful my great friend, Rocío, would be able to come in from Spain for the big day. (She was a Spanish exchange student my senior year of high school and we had become very close. Her family is like my own.) After a few weeks of planning, she called and confirmed that she would be honored to be a bridesmaid. She followed it up by saying her husband, Jaume, and parents, Gloria and Salvador, as well as her Aunt Teresa, would all be joining her for the trip. I cried. I couldn't believe they would make the trip from Spain for our wedding day. Wow! *My cup runneth over.*

Other things like guest lists, invitations, favors, decorations, flowers, pictures (my roommate Keri was the photographer), playlists (Luke and Levi were DJs), and cakes (yes, cakes with an *s*, my Mom made thirty cakes as center pieces for each table) all came together in time. The week of the wedding arrived, and many friends came into town early to join in the celebration. (This included Rocío and her family). We had the annual Grice reunion picnic on July 3rd at the farm after rehearsing for the ceremony.

Since July 4th was on a Sunday, both Andy and I attended our home churches in the morning. I felt strongly that it was what the Lord wanted—to put Him first and honor the Sabbath. Meghan did my hair afterward, and we were off to St. Clairsville around lunch time.

The ceremony was at 2:30PM and it went by so quickly. I'm thankful for many great pictures to help us remember it. We had about 350 people of all ages in attendance and we filled the entire sanctuary. We wanted everyone we knew to come celebrate God's goodness with us. Dad was all smiles as he met me to walk down the aisle and give me away to be Andy's bride. Our friends, Lance and Nathan, led everyone in worship then onto prayer, vows (which we had written; see appendix), exchanging of the rings, communion for the two of us, laying on of hands (prayer of friends), the kiss, and finally the announcement of Mr. and Mrs. Nelson. (My Aunt Carol played the "Hallelujah Chorus" on piano as we parted.) The ceremony was a great gift and we are very thankful for the Lord's blessings upon it.

After many pictures were taken in the church, Levi drove us to the red covered bridge nearby where we had driven on a few dates. We got some great pictures there, and that bridge will always be a good memory for us. We didn't waste too much time, however, since we needed to get to the reception for dinner.

The whole day seemed to pass by in the blink of an eye. The reception was a lot of fun as we ate, danced, and spent time with our favorite people. I was grateful to Andy's leadership on deciding not to have alcohol at the reception. The milk (chocolate, white, and vanilla) provided by Schneider's Dairy (and Dad's farm) was just what was needed. We did a handful of country line dances to get everyone on their feet, and I was sure to wear my red cowboy boots to motivate others more. Andy, Luke, Levi, and Andy's friend, George, all surprised me by performing a disco dance to the song *Stayin' Alive*. It was one of my favorite things about the day. Andy even did a back flip. I think my family was in shock seeing quiet Andy on the dance floor with so much life.

It seemed like everyone had a great time before many headed out to meet family or watch Independence Day fireworks on the riverbanks in Wheeling. Jaume, Rocio, Andy and I all watched fireworks together on the river near the hotel. As the finale finished, we headed back to say goodbye to my parents and family before making our way to my Honda and the first stop of the honeymoon adventure. The whole day went perfectly, and I couldn't have asked for anything more.

The remainder of the summer was spent saying goodbyes and packing up to head to Langfang, China, for our first year of marriage. Those early months of marriage were really good to teach me about respect, forgiveness, patience, intimacy, and how Christ loves us through our spouse. It's a powerful thing… this *call* to marriage. I'm grateful that the Lord says in Matthew 18:20, *For where two or three come together in my name, there am I with them.* Isn't this great? The Lord is with us in marriage too! …*a cord of three strands is not quickly broken.* Ecclesiastes 4:12. Praise the Lord! Thank you, Jesus!

EPILOGUE I
(WRITTEN IN 2012)

Andy and I spent two years in China, teaching Oral English to students at Langfang Teachers College (a place we had visited the year prior as you may remember) and sharing the love of Christ. Afterward, we returned to the states to begin the next part of our adventure with the Lord—I was newly pregnant.

My life verse has always been 1 Thessalonians 5:16, *"Be joyful always."* I think what's impressed me most about Andy's spiritual life is his heart for prayer. It's neat that my favorite verse is followed by 1 Thessalonians 5:17, *"pray continually."* The exciting conclusion to those verses is in 18 *"give thanks in all circumstances, for this is God's will for you in Christ Jesus."* I always wondered what God's will was for my life, and here it is found in His word as a part of my life verse. A friend of ours recently pointed out if I were not doing God's will of *being joyful,* Andy might not have noticed me in 2002. It's a great blessing for both Andy and me to humbly try to live our lives as grateful people in all circumstances...for this is God's will for us... and it's His will for you too.

I've titled this book <u>Red Flower, Green Leaf</u> for multiple reasons, but also because it reminds me of the above-mentioned verses. What *joy* there is in seeing beautiful red flowers bloom? And isn't there a sense the bloom (*joy*) is cared for and nurtured by the green leaf (that *prays*)? It's God that works everything out for his good plan, including flowers. Shouldn't we give thanks for his perfect plan and provision that starts with Him as our root and stem?

You are fearfully and wonderfully made and just be patient.

EPILOGUE II
(WRITTEN IN 2023)

Andy and I were blessed with a couple precious boys and continued to work for Young Life and teach/sub at public schools after our return from China. In January of 2016 our third son (he was six weeks old) was admitted to the Pediatric Intensive Care Unit with RSV. It was one of the scariest weeks of our lives. In Andy's cry to the Lord for help he was sent to a Bible passage that said *preach the word*. Our son's health improved, and our trajectory in life moved from YL/teaching/parenting to working toward becoming a pastor full time. Andy began work as a Youth Director at a larger church in Fishers, Indiana, while taking seminary classes until February of 2020 when the Lord once again was putting it on his heart to pastor. After our fifth son was born in 2020 (amidst the COVID restrictions) we were sent to upstate New York as missionaries with Village Missions to *preach the word and love the people*. We are now in the process of an international adoption. We continue to share God's story of faithfulness to us from the early days of singleness to the recent days of parenting and marriage. *He* is the best Author.

APPENDIX A

I have kept all the cards and letters from those sweet dating years. Rereading them brings back many memories and ignites our marriage again. Much like the many letters (epistles) in the New Testament which were written in love and faith and continue to ignite our relationship with the Lord.

APPENDIX B

Letter I received on January 20, 2010

Currently it's 2:41PM on January 19, 2010, and I'm waiting for you to come home so that we can celebrate one year of being together! I have big plans for this evening. The biggest of those plans is asking you to marry me. Thinking of marrying you brings a smile to me.

Thanks for loving Jesus and being so wonderful throughout this period of 'Andy and Heather Pre-engagement'. You've often thanked me for pursuing you. Yet, I forget to thank you for being so God-dependent through the past two years which makes our story what it is. You could have said yes a long time ago without much thought to prayer and what God wanted for us. If you would have done that, we may still be together but our story would have been different.

For me, it's been so right to put on armor, so to speak, and fight for you. I want to continue pursuing your heart and spending time with you. I look forward to all that Jesus has for us!

I love you! You're beautiful! God is good, Heather! My cup overflows. Love, Andy

APPENDIX C

Our Wedding Vows

Andy wrote...

"Heather, you are so beautiful. You are fearfully and wonderfully made. I remember the first time I saw you. You were with your friends laughing and I could see the joy of the Lord in you! Today, I see not only joy, but peace, patience, kindness, goodness, faithfulness, generosity, hope and love. You are amazing! I am a better person because of you. You're the best and I love you! **

And so with this ring I make you a promise today. I promise, with God's help, to cherish you, care for you, serve you, lead you, and love you for as long as we both shall live. Today, I commit to loving you as Christ loved the church and gave Himself up for her. Heather, please accept this ring as a symbol of the vows we are taking today as we enter into the sacred and special gift of marriage."

**It was at this time during our wedding ceremony that Chris Buda (who married us) told me to go ahead and kiss Andy because words like those deserve a kiss. It's not every bride that gets to kiss her groom twice during the ceremony!

Heather wrote...

"I love you, Andy, and it seems I love you more with each day. Thank you for trusting Jesus with your life and putting your faith in me as your bride. You're my best friend and the finest example I know of someone who walks humbly with our God. I respect and admire you so much! I'm proud of you and excited to be your wife and helpmate and share our lives together.

With this ring as a symbol, I promise before God who brought us together, to love you, care for you, encourage you, believe in you, pray for you, be faithful to you and follow you through all of life's experiences as you follow God."

APPENDIX D

<u>Reflection Questions and Verses</u>

1. **Love**

   What part of Heather's love story can you relate to most and why? Have you fallen in love yet with the One who will never fail you, who pursues you, and is always there for you (Jesus, your Bridegroom)? Are you trusting Him with the love story He has planned for you—using your single days to draw near to God and others He puts before you? Why or why not?

   "For God so loved the world that he gave his one and only Son, that whoever believes in him shall not perish but have eternal life." *John 3:16*

2. **Faithfulness**

   Where did you see Andy or Heather take a faith step (where they trusted in God to work something out)? What faith steps have you already taken in your life? Where do you need to trust God for something new that He's doing right now?

   "Then Jesus told him, "Because you have seen me, you have believed; blessed are those who have not seen and yet believed."" *John 20:29*

3. **Prayer**

   What were some prayers that were answered for Heather or Andy? What prayers have you already seen God answer in your life? What are some prayers that you need to be more intentional to pray over this next week, month, or year?

"If you remain in me and my words remain in you, ask whatever you wish, and it will be given you." John 15:7

4. **Share**

   Consider memorizing one of the verses mentioned in *Red Flower, Green Leaf.* Write it below or on a separate sheet of paper then share it with someone who may need some encouragement. *Thank you for sharing your time with me. Love, Heather :)*

ACKNOWLEDGEMENTS

There are so many people that played a role in this book. Some are mentioned and some are not. Still others played an invaluable part in our story and we never knew their names. This is the humbling part of walking in faith with Jesus each day...You never know what God will do or who you will meet.

Big thanks to:

> **You**-for reading this story of how God works in the hearts of men and women. He is in every detail, and it's no coincidence that you are reading this. I'm praying for you. Be patient in the love story He wants to give you. Honor Him in your waiting and/or singleness by serving Him, loving Him, and learning more about Him.

> **Andy**, who has always been encouraging and supportive in this endeavor (as well as chief editor). You are a better story teller than me, and I've learned so much from you. I love you deeply.

> **My sons,** who allowed me to sit and edit countless hours while they played around me.

> **Marlene Speidel** (our German daughter/exchange student), who was the first teenager to read it and enjoy it (in 2016). We love you like our own.

My parents, siblings, in-laws, family and friends who love me so well. I love you back!

Vonda Cranfield, who read it in one sitting and told me it needed to be published. Thank you!

Hilary Hrutkay, a childhood friend, gifted in all things editing/ Word (as well as hospitality). Thanks for the late-night cookies and editing session!

Young Life, Youth for Christ, and ***Village Missions***-ministries that are near and dear to my heart for so many reasons.

Jesus Christ, for it's by Him that "we know what love is: Jesus Christ laid down his life for us…" 1 John 3:16.

Printed in the United States
by Baker & Taylor Publisher Services